CU00924369

THIS PRESENT EMERGENCY

THIS PRESENT EMERGENCY

EDINBURGH, THE RIVER FORTH AND SOUTH-EAST SCOTLAND
AND THE SECOND WORLD WAR

by ANDREW JEFFREY

MAINSTREAM
PUBLISHING

EDINBURGH AND LONDON

Copyright © Andrew Jeffrey, 1992

All rights reserved.

The moral right of the author has been asserted
First published in Great Britain in 1992 by
MAINSTREAM PUBLISHING COMPANY (EDINBURGH) LTD
7 Albany Street
Edinburgh EH1 3UG

ISBN 1 85158 506 0

No part of this book may be reproduced or transmitted in any form
or by any other means without the permission in writing from the
publisher, except by a reviewer who wishes to quote brief passages
in connection with a review written for insertion in a magazine,
newspaper or broadcast.

A catalogue record for this book is available from the British
Library.

Typeset in 11/12 Sabon by WEPS Electronic Publishing Systems,
Cockenzie.
Printed in Great Britain by Martins the Printers Ltd, Berwick Upon
Tweed.

Ref. No._____

AUXILIARY AIR FORCE

NOTICE OF CALLING OUT

under the

Reserve and Auxiliary Forces Act, 1939

Name _____ *Ross, H. T.* _____

Rank _____ *Lac.* _____ Number _____ *8033/6* _____ No. 803 City of Edinburgh **Squadron**

Unit _____

Following Directions given by the Secretary of State in accordance with an Order by His Majesty in Council, made under Section 1 (1) of the above-mentioned Act, you are as a member of the Auxiliary Air Force called out for service ~~during the~~ period_____ to _____ ~~both dates inclusive.~~

You are hereby required to attend at_____ **R.A.F. STATION, TURNHOUSE**

~~not later than~~ *immediately* o'clock on the first date above mentioned. Should you not present ~~yourself as ordered~~ you will be liable to be proceeded against.

Date_____

[stamp: TURNHOUSE 23 AUG 1939 EDINBURGH, 112 AUXILIARY AIR FORCE]

_____ Adjutant

Unit ____ 803 City of Edinburgh **Squadron,**

Auxiliary Air Force

INSURANCE CARDS AND UNEMPLOYMENT BOOKS.

If you are subject to the National Health Insurance and Unemployment Insurance Acts, you are required to bring your card and book with you when joining.

(2851) Wt. 17202—1090 5,000 Pads 6/39 T.S. 700

Contents

Chapter One

Ready For Action

'The war's on, the war's on - you'd better go home and get your gas mask!'

Admonition to children playing in the street at Haymarket in Edinburgh at around 1120 hours, Sunday, 3 September 1939.

Five Whistles Bend loomed out of the early morning mist clinging to the River Vistula. At 0447 hours on Friday, 1 September 1939, Kapitan zur see Gustav Kleikamp gave the order to open fire and the 11-inch guns of the old battleship *Schleswig Holstein* sent their shells screaming into the Polish military transit depot at Westerplatte. The Second World War had begun.

Later that morning John Inglis, the King's and Lord Treasurer's Remembrancer, entered the Crown Room at Edinburgh Castle along with representatives of Brook and Son, the Royal jewellers. With great care, they packed the Scottish Crown Jewels into wooden boxes which they placed inside a large wooden chest. This was removed to a vault under the Crown Room, where it was placed in a recess, covered with a layer of sandbags and padlocked behind a fireproof door.

The war-warning signal, 'DIABOLO', had been received at RAF Turnhouse on 24 August. By that evening, 603 (City of Edinburgh) Squadron of the Auxiliary Air Force had dispersed their Gladiator fighters around the airfield perimeter. Gun batteries around the Forth were ordered to fuse their shells at 0100 hours on 25 August and those at Inchgarvie, Pettycur and Kinghorn reported 'ready for action' at 1250 hours the following day. Naval examination vessels left to take up their stations at 1815 hours on Friday 1 September and, at 0730 hours on the 3rd, the air operations control room at Donibristle warned units to 'Expect hostile action from 0930 hours'.

Air-Raid Precautions personnel had been placed on call that Friday night and the blackout was in force. On Saturday, Hearts beat Motherwell 4-2 and queues formed early to see John Wayne in *Stagecoach*. That evening, it was announced that there would be no more firings of the one o' clock gun from Edinburgh Castle 'until further notice'.

Detailed planning for the evacuation of children from Edinburgh and Rosyth had begun early in 1939. That April 33,150 households in the capital took part in a survey designed to assess the level of

ERI evacuation. In anticipation of massive numbers of casualties arising from enemy air attacks within hours of the declaration of war, hospitals, including Edinburgh Royal Infirmary seen here, were cleared of patients. Those suffering from TB were asked not to cough on children.
Nobody seems to have considered the fact that the Luftwaffe had few aircraft capable of reaching and effectively bombing the city, and that most of those were otherwise occupied in Poland.
(LOTHIAN HEALTH BOARD ARCHIVES)

interest but only 12,642 families, with around 37,000 children, indicated a wish to take part in the official scheme. Meanwhile, Edinburgh's City Analyst was examining various makes of biscuit to determine which was the most wholesome for issue to evacuees. In the event, the Corporation bought the cheapest.

A leaflet circulated to parents in July 1939 was at once both reassuring and alarmist. Entitled '*Evacuation - Why and How*', it urged parents not to let their children experience the dangers and fears of an air attack in crowded cities. At the same time, it stated that 'our defences are strong'. John Colville, Secretary of State for Scotland, commented that the leaflet went too far in encouraging people to participate in the voluntary government scheme. There was simply not enough accommodation in the receiving areas.

Though mothers and children with friends in the country had been leaving the city for some days, the official evacuation scheme got under way early on Friday, 1 September 1939. Optimistic press reports stated that just over 30,000 had left the city by the following evening but noted that even that total was considerably less than the numbers who had expressed an interest six months earlier. In fact, as Education Department records show, the actual figure was even lower. Only 26,000 had left the city, just over 40 per cent of those eligible to take part. By March 1940, and despite the fact that as many as 100 children were still being sent out of the city every week, there were only 8,829 children in official reception areas. Some 1,139 were to be found 'elsewhere'. By March 1941 a mere 4,118 children and 128 teachers were scattered from Inverness, to Clackmannan, to the Borders. Of the 755 mothers and children evacuated from Rosyth, 407 had returned by Christmas 1939.

Two evacuation camps were constructed, one at Broomlee, West Linton, and the other at Middleton, Gorebridge. Each was designed to hold 360 children aged between eight and 12 and provide at least three-and-a-half hours of schooling every day. The first 94 children arrived at Broomlee on 22 April 1940, four days before it was opened by John Colville. An early report from the headmaster bemoans a serious lack of facilities. 'The pitiful attempts made by the children to skate or trundle hoops on the narrow concrete paths are very disheartening for all who wish to see them really happy.'

Winter weather at the camp revealed chronic drainage problems. The flooded play area became known as the 'Black Sea' as it was churned into mud. It was used for sailing toy boats. Urgent appeals for something to be done were ignored though the Education Committee did supply the children with clogs, which staff described as 'a godsend'. A much more serious problem arose from children being visited by their families carrying inner city diseases such as measles.

The poor response to the evacuation scheme created a considerable problem in the city. Pre-war shelter building, limited as it was, had concentrated on domestic and public shelters. Schools had largely been ignored, and those without shelters were forced to close. In addition, a considerable amount of school accommodation had been taken over by the Air-Raid Precautions services for use as first-aid posts, warden's posts, rest centres and gas cleansing centres. Literally thousands of children were left to roam the streets and delinquency increased at an alarming rate. Desperate parents were encouraged by the Education Department to organise classes for small groups of children in each others homes. As late as March 1940, seven months into the war, 33,791 children had returned to school in the city, leaving 9,513 still reliant on some form of group instruction. Two thousand seven hundred and thirty were not attending any form of schooling whatsoever and were largely to be found in full-time employment.

Official policy on evacuation had, from the start, been based on the assumption that the poorer, or 'priority evacuation classes', would panic under air attack. Yet the Scottish Home and Health Department piously expected parents to provide evacuee children with, among other things, handkerchiefs, a tooth brush, a face cloth, pyjamas and house shoes or rubber shoes, items most inner-city children would never have set eyes on. Publicity showing relatively well-to-do Edinburgh children attending school at Scone Palace failed to conceal the magnitude of the culture-clash which had occurred. The true scale of loathsome inner-city decay and deprivation was, for the first time, forcibly brought home to the middle and upper classes. Reaction was mixed, not least among relatively well-off housewives who suddenly found themselves having to cope with verminous children and contagious skin diseases. As the figures of those returning to the inner cities show, this first attempt at bridging the social divide resulted in both sides recoiling with much to think about.

A second mass evacuation took place after the heavy raids on Clydeside in 1941. Six hundred and forty children were accommodated in Larbert Central School in the week after much of Clyde-bank was destroyed in March. Two months later, further raids brought 2,170 children from Hyndland and Drumchapel by bus and train to Stirling, from where the Chief Billeting Officer was forced to ask for assistance from the Chief Sanitary Inspector in Glasgow. Completely out of their depth, records show the Scottish

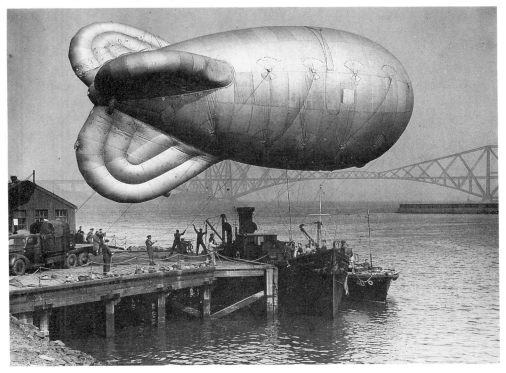

Barrage Balloon.

Barrage balloons were in very short supply at the outbreak of war and it was not until 1703 hours on 18 October 1939, two days after the Forth Raid, that the first balloon was flown by 929 (Barrage Balloon) Squadron from the south side of Dalmeny School. Seven, as here, were mounted on ships moored in the river.

Twelve balloons were destroyed when an electrical storm coincided with an alert on 6 July 1940. Admiral Ramsay, the Flag Officer Rosyth, wrote: 'Considering the nearest enemy aircraft plot was in the Kelso area, it was a pretty expensive twelve minutes' work.'

(603 SQUADRON ARCHIVES)

Office to have concerned itself more with what it termed 'moral and spiritual welfare' of the children.

Children were not the only ones leaving Edinburgh in that last weekend of peace. For the previous week trains had been packed with men in uniform as the reserve forces reported for duty, prisoners with less than three months to serve were cleared out of Scotland's jails and many of the treasures of the National Gallery were moved to Innerleithen in Peeblesshire.

The Soviet Union had signed an alliance with Germany, and Poland had been invaded and Neville Chamberlain sonorously informed the nation that it was a bitter blow to him that all his efforts to win peace had failed. For many of the generation who would have to do the fighting and the dying, Chamberlain's words appeared nothing if not self-serving. Followed shortly afterwards by an even more irresolute France, Britain was a nation at war. As one Edinburgher, then with his parents at a holiday camp in Rothesay, remembers, 'The women cried, and the men went home'. Immediately after the Prime Minister had finished speaking, Stirling Town Council requested a military guard on the streets, 'in the interest of public order'.

As to the Crown Jewels, in 1941 rumours started that they were to be sent overseas for safety. The Act of Union of 1706 specifically forbids their removal from Scotland and on 12 May 1942, Brook and Sons were back in the vault under the Crown Room in Edinburgh Castle. Mr Brook placed the regalia into two zinc-lined cases which were then soldered shut. One of the cases was walled up deep inside an archaeological excavation shaft in Tank Room no 1 under the Half Moon Battery. The other was buried under the floor of a garde-robe in an adjoining room. Four copies of the location plans were prepared. The Secretary of State for Scotland, Tom Johnstone MP, received one as did the King's and Lord Treasurer's Remembrancer. A copy was sent to the King and, prior to being despatched to a bank vault in Canada, the fourth copy was sealed in an envelope which bore the following inscription:

'SECRET, SCOTTISH REGALIA. TO BE DESTROYED IF IN DANGER OF SEIZURE BY THE ENEMY.'

Chapter Two

'By Gosh, That's Like Bombing!'

Lieutenant Inglis stared skywards in astonishment. Engines scream-ing, a black bomber was diving out of a clear sunlit sky. Two bombs fell fróm the aircraft and exploded between two cruisers lying at anchor east of the Forth Bridge. It was 1435 hours on Monday, 16 October 1939. The first attack on the British Isles of the Second World War had begun.

The opening shots of the air war over Britain had been fired that morning. At 0945 the Observer Corps reported an unidentified aircraft moving south-west over Dunfermline. Three minutes later the Spitfires of Blue Section, 602 (City of Glasgow) Squadron roared across the grass at RAF Drem near North Berwick.

The enemy aircraft was in fact one of a pair of reconnaissance Heinkels from Kampfgeschwader 26. It flew over the Naval docky-ard at Rosyth where it took photographs before heading for home, passing over the bridge at 1008 hours. At 1021 hours, it was intercepted near May Island by 602's Spitfires. Blue Leader and Renfrewshire farmer, Flight Lieutenant George Pinkerton, earned the distinction of being the first pilot to go into action against the Luftwaffe with a Spitfire. In addition, when he and his number two, Flying Officer Archie McKellar, chased the Heinkel into cloud, they fired the first shots of the air war over the British Isles. Pinkerton fired 720 rounds and McKellar 1,000. The enemy aircraft was last seen hastening eastwards around 20 miles east of Dunbar.

Indications of enemy activity from both intercepted radio traffic and occasional sightings of high-flying aircraft continued for the rest of the morning. At 1120 hours, another reconnaissance Heinkel was sighted over Drem. 602's Commanding Officer, Glasgow stockbroker Douglas Farquhar was told, rather casually, that he could investigate if he thought it necessary. Needing little encouragement, Red Section were off the ground two minutes later but the Heinkel had made off to the south east. It was last seen circling the 360-foot masts of the radar station at Drone Hill, south of Cockburnspath, before heading out to sea.

The Chain Home radar station at Drone Hill was part of a network, hastily installed during 1939, which stretched around the south and east coasts of Britain from Devon to Caithness. Fighter Command's command and control network was heavily dependent on the ability of radar to detect hostile aircraft up to 80 miles out to sea. This allowed the best use to be made of the small number of modern aircraft that were available for home defence. Radar was, however, still in its infancy and was notoriously unreliable. At 0949 hours that morning, just as Pinkerton led his section off from Drem, Drone Hill reported the first of two breakdowns which would have a crucial effect on the day's events. RAF Sector Controllers at Turnhouse had been blinded in one eye. Now there was only the Observer Corps.

With their radar cover inoperative, Sector Control at RAF Turnhouse appears to have become beset by confusion. Green Section of 602 Squadron, scrambled from Drem at 1045 hours, were sent in quick succession to Dunbar, back to give top cover at Drem, out to sea and finally, after refuelling back at Drem, north towards Montrose. Eventually, it was realised that plotting errors had sent many of the patrols on reciprocal courses, directly away from unidentified aircraft. Enemy activity lessened by lunchtime and, apart from standing patrols, the Spitfires were recalled to refuel.

The Luftwaffe airfield at Sylt on the island of Westerland was, prior to the invasion of Norway and Denmark, their closest base to the Forth. There, Hauptman Helmut Pohle was in command of the brand new Junkers 88 (JU 88) bombers of the first wing of Kampfgeschwader 30 (1/KG30). KG 30 had been the first unit to receive the JU 88 and great things were expected from the Luftwaffe's new 'wonder bomber'. On 26 September, aircraft of Pohle's unit had taken part in the first attack on ships of the Royal Navy. During that, from the German point of view, unsuccessful action, a Sea Skua piloted by Lieutenant B. S. McEwan from 803 Squadron in HMS *Ark Royal* brought down a Dornier 18 flying boat, the first

In this remarkable Luftwaffe photograph a bomb has just exploded alongside HMS Southampton (left), sinking her pinnace and the Admiral's barge. The up-turned hull of the latter drifted towards the bridge and was thought by some to be wreckage from a crashed enemy aircraft.

(TRUSTEES OF THE IMPERIAL WAR MUSEUM, LONDON)

German aircraft to fall to British guns in the Second World War. Another Dornier was claimed by a Hudson of 224 Squadron from Leuchars following combat 20 miles north-east of Aberdeen on 8 October 1939.

On 16 October, Pohle's orders were to find and attack the battlecruiser HMS *Hood*, thought to be on her way to Rosyth. His instructions were explicit on one thing; he was not to attack the ship if she was in dock as the German High Command still harboured the hope that all-out war could be averted and were determined to avoid civilian casualties.

At 1415 hours, as Pohle led his scattered formation towards the Forth estuary, the radar operators at Drone Hill were wrestling with their second breakdown of the day. Their equipment was out of action owing to a failure of the public electricity supply. They had no emergency generators. At that moment, the audience in Dunfermline's Regal Cinema were settling into their seats for a matinee performance of *Jesse James*, 'in glorious Technicolor' starring Tyrone Power. Meanwhile, Green Section of 602 Squadron were refuelling at Leuchars. They had spent the previous hour chasing non-existent enemy aircraft as far north as Montrose.

The first confirmation of enemy aircraft in the East Lothian area came from the Observer Corps at 1420 hours. George Pinkerton and Blue Section were immediately scrambled to patrol Dalkeith at 20,000 feet and were off the ground three minutes later.

In Dalmeny Park the crew of anti-aircraft battery RSG 1 were practising loading drill. At 1427 hours the Battery Commander reported a Junkers 88 flying up the river. At 1430 hours, not unnaturally keen to open fire on an enemy bomber clearly intent on evil deeds, he reported the Junkers to be immediately over the Forth Bridge. Indecision appears to have gripped his superiors and he was not given the order to open fire until a full 11 minutes after his first enemy aircraft report and three minutes after the first bombs had been dropped.

Intense, though friendly, rivalry existed between the Glasgow Auxiliary Squadron and their neighbours, 603 (City of Edinburgh) Squadron. 603 were operating from their home base at RAF Turnhouse and had exchanged their obsolete Gladiator biplane fighters for new Spitfires only a few days earlier. At 1430 hours, just as Helmut Pohle was arriving over the Forth Bridge, Flight Lieutenant Patrick 'Patsy' Gifford in XT-A led Red Section off towards the river. They were followed almost immediately by Flight Lieutenant George Denholm who led Yellow Section off in response to Observer Corps reports of unidentified aircraft moving westwards over Dalkeith. It was Denholm's section which made first contact with the enemy formation. No sooner had the Spitfires left the ground than a searchlight crew watched as they ran into a flight of three bombers at around 4,000 feet over Threipmuir Reservoir. Earlier, at 1435 hours, Constable James Henderson at Roslin had watched one of the bombers making its way to the west and, almost immediately, heard gunfire. One minute later he saw a bomber being chased over the village by Denholm's fighters. At Langhill Farm, north of the village, Joseph Thomson was showered in cartridge cases as aircraft roared low over his farmhouse. At Swanston Cottages near Hillend, Herbert More saw two of the bombers coming under attack from Spitfires before they disappeared into a bank of low cloud. The fight was also witnessed by another Hillend resident who told an Evening News reporter that he had seen one of the bombers making off in a north-easterly direction towards Auchendinny.

It was this aircraft which blundered, at 4,000 feet, into Pat Gifford and Red Section who were returning, empty-handed, from a patrol towards Haddington. At Carberry Hill, Gifford's Spitfires came on the scene with what one onlooker described as 'a terrific roar'. As they manoeuvred to attack, the bomber veered sharply to port, setting a course north towards the Forth. When Gifford, Ken McDonald and Colin Robertson attacked, pieces were observed falling off the aircraft and one engine was put out of action. Children in Cockenzie School were startled by the sound of gunfire as aircraft roared overhead.

John Dickson was quite unaware of the raid as he brought his 35-foot line fishing yawl *Dayspring* back to Port Seton from the fishing grounds off May Island. With his two sons, William and John, along with Sandy and Andrew Harkness, he enjoyed an unrivalled view as Pat Gifford delivered the final attack on the Junkers. With smoke pouring out, it reared up before crashing into the sea about four miles offshore.

At first Dickson was less than enthusiastic about rescuing the survivors who could be clearly seen in the water. He thought they might be armed and would try to hijack his boat in an attempt to get back to Germany. His elder son William was even less enthusiastic, believing that the German crew might have bombed Edinburgh and killed people. No seaman will knowingly leave someone to drown, however, and the fishermen quickly forgot their misgivings. Hastening to the crash site, they picked up three survivors as another Junkers passed low overhead. The body of rear-gunner Obergefrieter Krämer was not found.

Contemporary newspaper reports contain lurid tales of supposed injuries suffered by the survivors. In fact, apart from cuts and bruises, none was seriously injured, although one of them, 27-year-old Feldwebel Hans Georg Hielscher, who was due to be married the following January, had taken a knock in the ribs. All of them managed to walk unaided up the harbour steps when the *Dayspring* reached Port Seton half an hour later. Oberleutnant Hans Storp, the pilot, told a German-speaking local that, 'we had no chance to get away . . . our plane was just too slow'. As a mark of his gratitude for saving his life, he gave John Dickson a gold ring which his son still wears. Pieces of wreckage found floating near the crash site became much prized souvenirs. From Port Seton Police Station, where they received first-aid from local GP Dr Black, Storp, Hielscher and Feldwebel Hugo Rohnke were taken, under escort, to the military hospital in Edinburgh Castle.

Arriving over the bridge at 1430 hours Helmut Pohle looked in vain for HMS *Hood*. He did see a large warship in Rosyth but German intelligence had been in error; this was HMS *Repulse*. Mindful of his instruction not to attack vessels in the dockyard,

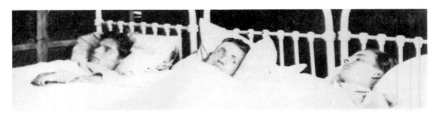

Hans Storp, Hugo Rohnke and Hans Georg Heilscher in the military hospital at Edinburgh Castle.

Storp was later interrogated by a panel which included a somewhat absent-minded scientist from the famous code-breaking centre at Bletchley Park. In his book, Most Secret War, Professor R. V. Jones writes of the panel's efforts to establish their superiority over the prisoner. They were seated behind a long table, the door was thrown open and Storp marched in. On reaching the centre of the room he came smartly to attention and threw up his arm in an immaculate Nazi salute. Immediately, the absent-minded code-breaker leapt to his feet, threw his arm up in a Nazi salute and returned Storp's 'Heil Hitler!' Realising he had committed an awful gaffe, he then sat down in such a hurry that he completely missed his chair and landed in a heap on the floor.

(AUTHOR'S COLLECTION)

possibly causing civilian casualties, he decided to bomb the two cruisers moored off South Queensferry. Wasting no time, he tipped the Junkers into a dive. As the bomber screamed steeply downwards, a design fault revealed itself with a loud bang as the cockpit canopy flew off.

At North Queensferry, Adam McMahon was one of a number of workmen building air-raid shelters beneath the arches of the bridge. He had seen the bombers approach along the north shore of the river and watched as Pohle circled over Rosyth. The explosion of Pohle's two bombs at 1435 hours was followed by a third loud report as the door of an outside toilet was thrown back. An officer emerged and, seemingly unaware that his trousers were still draped around his ankles, started shouting orders to the soldiers guarding the bridge. At precisely the same moment Provost Walker of South Queensferry exclaimed to his wife, 'By gosh, that's like bombing!'

Having completed his attack and despite the fact that he was now flying an open aircraft, Pohle climbed out towards Inverkeithing to observe the results achieved by the rest of his unit. It was as the second Junkers attacked, at 1438 hours, that Dalmeny Park battery was at last given permission to open fire. The batteries at Dalmeny village, Donibristle, Mire End and Primrose Farm near Rosyth joined in almost immediately, and the sky filled with the white smoke of bursting shells.

As the action spread south-east over the city and west towards Bo'ness, shrapnel came raining down over a wide area. Traffic held up by police on the Hawes Brae was peppered and windows were broken in Inverkeithing, South Queensferry, Kirkliston, Granton and Portobello where one piece smashed through the window of a moving tram, narrowly missing a passenger. Territorials guarding the north end of the rail bridge had to duck behind the parapet as HMS *Repulse* added her considerable barrage to the fray, sending streams of lead whistling over their heads. In the city considerable quantities of shrapnel fell around Haymarket, in Rutland Square, Hanover Street, Fettes Row, St Andrew Square, Advocate's Close, Cockburn Street, East Fettes Avenue and Corstorphine, where the roof of the Home and Colonial Stores in St John's Road was damaged. A dog hit by splinters in Alma Street, Inverkeithing had to be destroyed and a woman standing at Dalmeny Station escaped injury when a red-hot shell splinter dropped into the pocket of her apron, setting it on fire. Several telephone wires were cut around

South Queensferry and 24-year-old Peter McGowan was slightly wounded in the back while working at Wheatlands Farm, Kirkliston. One large piece of shrapnel fell through the roof of the scullery at Couston Farm, Aberdour, slightly injuring the farmer's wife Mrs Milne.

Potentially lethal shell caps made of brass and lead were also crashing to earth. One landed only inches from a nursing sister at Edinburgh Royal Infirmary and another went through the roof of a laundry at Meadow Place. Yet another damaged a concrete path in the front garden at 24 Laverockbank Avenue, Trinity, and was still hot when handed to a passing policeman some minutes later. With commendable phlegm, Mrs Kenny asked him, 'Is this something they have left behind?' The fusing of shells in the early days of the war was a somewhat haphazard science and many dropped back to earth without exploding. They were found at Leuchold House in Dalmeny Park, on Almondhill Road and at the crossroads in Kirkliston. Another shell caused much concern when it was heard whizzing over Linlithgow to explode in a wood south of the town.

An additional problem for the gunners was that, during the early part of the raid, training aircraft from Donibristle were still unconcernedly buzzing around and generally getting in the way.

Shortly after George Denholm's section had intercepted the first flight of bombers at Threipmuir Reservoir, a further section of five enemy aircraft was observed approaching round the south of Edinburgh. Mr J. McGregor, the manager of the South Queensferry branch of the Clydesdale Bank, watched as the first three of these aircraft appeared over the town from the south-west and dived on the cruisers. On this occasion one bomb penetrated *Southampton*'s superstructure, passing through two lower decks to emerge through the hull above the water line. There it exploded, sinking a pinnace and the Admiral's barge which were lying at the boom.

During the first attack, a train to Dunfermline had halted at Dalmeny Station. By the time the second attack developed, the train was crossing the bridge and the passengers had an unrivalled view as the Junkers swooped low overhead to drop their bombs.

On taking off from Drem at 1423 hours George Pinkerton, Archie McKellar and Paul Webb of 602 Squadron began the slow climb to their allotted patrol point at 20,000 feet over Dalkeith. Minutes later they were diverted to Tranent, whereupon Pinkerton received the signal: 'Enemy aircraft bombing Rosyth. Patrol five miles north of present position'. On taking up their new position, they first set off after two aircraft seen by Archie McKellar. These, however, turned out to be more of the Sea Skua training aircraft from Donibristle, which were spending the afternoon getting in everyone's way. Exasperated, George Pinkerton led his section after an enemy aircraft he had earlier seen making east past Kirkcaldy.

With a jubilant 'Villa Blue Section . . . Tally Ho . . . Buster,' Pinkerton ordered his section into line astern. Sweeping round onto the Junkers' tail, they passed through a bank of cloud in which Paul Webb became disorientated and lost contact with his comrades. A few seconds later, the enemy aircraft appeared from cloud and he ordered McKellar to follow him in attacking, in succession, from behind and above. The Observer Corps logged the sound of two aircraft firing at 1443 hours in the vicinity of Elie.

In the Junkers, Helmut Pohle struggled with the controls as he tried to shake off his assailants. But with Pinkerton on his starboard side and McKellar on his port, every time he took evasive action it only brought him into range of one of the faster and more manoeuvrable Spitfires. First, he reared up only 50 yards in front of Pinkerton, who poured a blizzard of fire from his eight Brownings into the Junkers. As Pohle attempted to dive away into cloud, McKellar attacked and damaged the bomber's wingtip. Pinkerton then hit the starboard engine and McKellar hit the port. As Pohle recalls, 'We could not defend ourselves with the rear top gun as it had gone with the canopy.' Two of his crew had been killed and his radio operator had been seriously wounded. Desperately, he hauled the control column back to avoid hitting a trawler. Then Pinkerton attacked again and, with both engines now out of action and the interior of the bomber a shambles, a crash was inevitable.

From Balcomie golf course at Fife Ness, greenkeeper Mr J. McNaughtan watched the stricken bomber make a final despairing lunge skywards before dropping 'like a stone' into the sea. In his combat report, Pinkerton gives the time of the combat as 'about 1500 hours'. Observer Corps post 36/B2 noted the crash as having taken place at 1455 hours, three miles east of Crail. A further eyewitness report, confirming the time and location of the crash, is appended to the Observer Corps log for the day.

Paul Webb, meanwhile, finding himself on his own east of May Island, engaged two other members of Pohle's flight. He chased

Pat Gifford is shown here as his Spitfire 'Stickleback' is refuelled immediately after landing at RAF Turnhouse from the successful action over Port Seton. He carried out two further patrols that afternoon.

Gifford, a solicitor from Castle Douglas with a weakness for fast cars, was posted to command 3 Squadron, a Hurricane unit, on 15 November 1939. One of the last entries in his logbook is dated 24 April 1940 and refers to a forced landing after his engine cut out at 500 feet. It merely says, 'Bit shaken, very lucky.' He was shot down and killed the following month.

(603 SQUADRON ARCHIVES)

them south-east to St Abbs Head before rejoining his section to land at Drem at 1515 hours.

A third wave of enemy bombers was seen crossing the coast at 1445 hours near Dunbar, heading first west and then south in the direction of Haddington. At precisely that moment the rural quiet of Turnhouse was shattered as, Merlin engines roaring, the six Spitfires of B Flight, 603 Squadron were scrambled to patrol North Berwick at 3,000 feet.

As the action intensified, there is some evidence of tension between the Turnhouse Sector Controller and his superiors at 13 Group, Fighter Command, who had overall responsibility for Scotland and Northern England. This is hardly surprising given that Fighter Command's tactics were being tested for the first time and, inevitably, flaws were appearing. The patrol orders to 603 Squadron were amended by Group with a terse 'B Flight too low at 3,000 feet, get them up to the correct height'.

In order to extend a line of fighters across East Lothian and the Forth, Control scrambled Red Section of 602 Squadron at 1451 hours to patrol over their base at Drem.

The next phase of the action fell to 602 Squadron. Shortly before 1500 hours, Flight-Lieutenant Dunlop Urie intercepted a bomber off Kirkcaldy which he pursued south-east over the river to St Abbs Head. It was last seen over Eyemouth with Urie still in hot pursuit. Pilot Officer Norman Stone, a solicitor from Whitecraigs near Glasgow, caught another near Gullane at 1510 which dived away to the east on being attacked. It was probably this aircraft which attracted the hostile attentions of some of 603's Spitfires shortly afterwards. Flight-Lieutenant Marcus Robinson made two attacks on a pair of enemy aircraft near Dalkeith at the same time and Pilot Officer Hector McLean reported having intercepted an enemy aircraft at 5,000 feet over May Island at 1530 hours. During the brief combat which ensued another Spitfire, probably one of 603's, almost collided with McLean, no doubt, as he recalls, to the considerable amusement of the German rear gunner.

Thirty miles to the north-east, at the Coastal Command base at Leuchars, Green Section of 602 Squadron were being refuelled after their abortive patrol towards Peterhead. Their existence seems to have slipped the minds of Sector Control at Turnhouse until, at 1453 hours, 13 Group Headquarters asked 'Do you still have a flight at Leuchars?' An immediate recall was ordered.

George Pinkerton.

Like many of the pre-war auxiliaries, Pinkerton first gained his category 'A' flying licence with the Scottish Flying Club before being commissioned into 602 Squadron. In April 1940, Douglas Farquhar was posted to be Station Commander at Martlesham Heath in Suffolk and Pinkerton took over command of the Squadron. Three months later he was posted to the Turnhouse Ops Room, handing over command of the Squadron to Sandy Johnstone.

Pinkerton went on to lead the Speke Wing flying nightfighters over Liverpool and, in 1942, took over the Merchant Ship Fighter Unit, training pilots whose Hurricanes were fired from rocket powered catapults fitted to the bows of merchant vessels. The increased availability of escort carriers made this somewhat hazardous practice obsolete, no doubt to the relief of pilots who, if out of range of land, were required to parachute from their aircraft near an escort vessel which would then pick them up. Promoted to Group Captain, Pinkerton then took over command of 56 Operational Training Unit at RAF Tealing near Dundee where his Wing-Commander, Flying, was none other than his old 602 comrade, Sandy Johnstone. (The story of RAF Tealing is told in 'This Dangerous Menace - Dundee and the River Tay at War' by the same author.)

(GROUP CAPTAIN GEORGE PINKERTON, OBE, DFC)

Douglas Farquhar, Sandy Johnstone and Ian Ferguson were just beginning a late lunch when the station went on alert. Grabbing sandwiches they made for a shelter only to find it already full. Rather than upset Brian Baker, the formidable Station Commander, by returning to the mess, they sat on the grass mound covering the shelter and contentedly munched their rolls. Completely unaware of the action already taking place over the Forth, they relaxed in the sunshine and watched some Blenheim light bombers passing towards Edinburgh. Having wandered over to the mess to find out what was going on, Douglas Farquhar came running back shouting, 'For Christ's sake get a move on, those aren't Blenheims - they're ruddy Germans!' Hurrying off to their aircraft, they were regaled with Brian Baker's trenchant opinions of Fighter Command in general, and 602 Squadron in particular.

The engine of Sandy Johnstone's aircraft had been started first. When he climbed in, it had overheated to such an extent that, when he pushed the throttle forward, it merely backfired, belched out a cloud of thick black smoke and promptly stopped. By the time he got going again his comrades were miles away to the south.

At Kincraig Point near Earlsferry, signals officer Captain Lamb was watching a convoy moving up-river towards the boom defence. He saw Farquhar and Ferguson pass overhead as they raced towards the bridge. No sooner had they gone than, at 1520 hours, an enemy aircraft appeared overhead, dived on the convoy and dropped bombs, one of which exploded less than fifty feet from HMS *Mohawk*, part of its destroyer escort. A lone Spitfire then came over from the north and opened fire on the bomber at extreme range. Johnstone recalls having to extricate himself from the unwelcome attentions of Naval anti-aircraft gunners while firing at long range on a bomber climbing out eastwards.

Mohawk suffered considerable damage as machine-gun fire showered her decks and deadly splinters perforated the quarter-inch steel plating of her hull throughout its 250-foot length. Three officers, including the First Lieutenant, and 13 men were killed by either machine-gun fire or splinters.

On her bridge, Commander Richard Jolly had been gravely wounded in the stomach. Despite this, he refused repeated requests to go below or allow himself to be attended to. Saying, 'Leave me - go and look after the others,' he brought his ship at high speed the 30 miles to Rosyth, a passage which lasted over one-and-a-quarter hours. During this time his voice became so weak that he could not make himself heard and his orders had to be repeated by the navigating officer, who was himself wounded. With *Mohawk* safely alongside Y berth, Jolly rang off main engines and immediately collapsed. He died less than five hours later.

Arriving in the area of the bridge, Douglas Farquhar's attention was drawn, by anti-aircraft fire, to an enemy aircraft approaching from the north-east. This was one of the three bombers he had earlier seen passing south of Leuchars and which had been tracked over Cupar and Markinch by the Observer Corps before approaching Rosyth. Surrounded by bursting shells, the enemy pilot could not have been aware that, from the garden of Broomhall near Limekilns, the Earl of Elgin was attempting to bring him down with rifle fire.

Chased west towards Bo'ness the Junkers dropped its load near the burnt-out wreck of the former naval depot ship HMS *Caledonia*, once the Cunard liner *Majestic*, before turning east towards the sea. Over Turnhouse Golf Course the bomber came under attack from a new and even more unlikely source. Manning a machine-gun post at Turnhouse airfield was 603 Squadron's padre, Reverend Rossie Brown. In reply to the comment, 'Padre, that was a very short burst you fired at that Hun', he is said to have replied, 'Yes, it passed too quickly out of my diocese!'

The chase continued over Davidson's Mains and the Northern General Hospital. At 9 The Green, Davidson's Mains, Emma Riddel and her mother, Julia Hargreaves, were cut by flying glass when bullets came through a window. At the Northern General, stray gunfire broke a number of windows in Wards 1, 2 and 10, the recreation room and the nurses' quarters. Thirty-one year-old John Ferry was struck in the leg while working on military installations at West Pilton.

Over Trinity, the bomber was assailed by anti-aircraft fire as the two Spitfires were seen to stay just out of range. Workmen building air-raid shelters above Granton Square shepherded local residents into those that were completed. Sweeping round high buildings in Leith, the bomber pilot desperately tried to shake off his pursuers. In Assembly Street, five-year-old Ian McGarrity heard the noise and glanced up to see the bomber pass over at rooftop height. Sensibly, he wasted no time in diving under a trailer parked at the side of the road.

After the action, Ian Ferguson reported that the bomber went slowly along the coast after he had fired two bursts at it over Portobello. The German aircraft was last seen hedge-hopping over East Lothian before going out to sea near North Berwick.

Back at the bridge, two more interceptions had been made. In the first, shortly before 1600 hours, Flying Officer 'Bolster' Boulter of 603 Squadron caught a bomber near Inverkeithing. Potato pickers at Spencerfield Farm watched as he chased it through anti-aircraft fire from Donibristle Battery and out to sea over Aberdour. Another bomber was caught very low over Rosyth by Pilot Officer Colin Robertson and Pilot Officer James 'Black' Morton of 603 Squadron who pursued it over Edinburgh. Eyewitnesses spoke of seeing the aircraft, seemingly very close together, and hearing the rattle of machine-gun fire. The combat continued over Raeburn Place and past the Royal Scots Club in Abercromby Place where a meeting was in progress. As the Junkers roared past the window, the Chairman uttered the immortal line, 'My God, that's a Jerry!'. After a moment's stunned silence the meeting continued as though nothing had happened.

Painters Frank Flynn and Joe McLuskie were working on the upstairs windows of 45 Abercorn Terrace, Portobello, when, with a deafening roar, the bomber barrelled along the street. Flynn recalled that, as it passed them, it was lower than the top of the steeple of St Philip's Church across the road. He told reporters, 'Just then my pal said, "Something has hit me", and the next minute he crumpled to the ground. I went down the steps to him and saw that blood was pouring from his waistcoat.' Joe McLuskie was rushed to Leith Hospital where he underwent an emergency operation to remove a bullet lodged next to his stomach.

Two bullets smashed through an upstairs front window at Lord Provost Henry Steele's house at 10 Hamilton Street, Portobello, damaging a display cabinet full of antique china. Alexander McMillan, the Provost's chauffeur, told of hearing bursts of gunfire and seeing the bomber with its pursuing fighters. Bullets, he said, seemed to be spraying down on the house. Nearby, at 7 Colliesdene Crescent, Mr H.F. Robertson found a bullet which had smashed its way through a bedroom window, pierced some bedclothes and ricochetted off a bedside table before ending up lying on a pillow. Houses in Morton Street and Joppa Road, Portobello, were also damaged and one woman found a bullet in her child's pram after the combat had passed over her garden.

By 1630 hours most of the pilots had returned to their bases, leaving Archie McKellar and Paul Webb on standing patrol over the bridge. Squadron Intelligence Officers then began assessing the day's claims. Eleven pilots submitted combat reports. Early claims were for one Heinkel 111 and one Dornier 215 destroyed. As Sandy Johnstone remembers, 'We never were much good at identification!' This increased to three shot down and one seen going out to sea with one engine not running. Return fire had damaged the camshaft casing of George Gilroy's Spitfire.

It was felt that enemy camouflage was considerably more effective than that of the RAF and some pilots said that anti-aircraft fire had been of considerable assistance in locating enemy aircraft. Interrogation of the survivors of the Port Seton crash had revealed that enemy morale was low as regards the Spitfire for which they were said to have a healthy respect.

13 Group Operational Record Book reveals much when it says that pilots were learning to compensate for the downward kick of the Spitfire when using their guns. Taking into account the fact that 603 Squadron alone used over 16,000 rounds for a score of one shot down and one damaged, marksmanship was unquestionably poor. Pilots were however handicapped by outmoded tactics evolved for bi-plane fighters and by a Fighter Command directive which stated that their guns should be adjusted to operate at a range of 400 yards. By the following spring, many pilots were operating with their guns harmonised for 200 yards or even less, thus ensuring a heavier punch.

A Luftwaffe communique released the following day claims that two fighters were shot down by the bombers. It also states that its bombers were flying low enough for their crews to see 'Scottish peasants waving to them'.

Press coverage of the raids reveals something of the excitement felt at the time. Before the war, pundits and respected science fiction writers including H. G. Wells had prophesied that British cities would be devastated in one massive knock-out blow from the air. Initial euphoria that little damage had been done was soon replaced by recrimination. Central to this was the fact that no air-raid warning had sounded within Edinburgh. The Edinburgh *Evening News* fanned the flames of discontent by alleging that sirens had sounded in Perth and some districts of Fife. This was quite untrue as nowhere had orders been given to sound public sirens. What had happened was that military bases had gone on alert as soon as the raid began and the sound of their sirens had encouraged civilians living nearby to go to the shelters. At Port Edgar the local siren had sounded three minutes after the first bomb dropped, but only after the siren at Rosyth had been clearly heard across the river. This was followed by the frenzied screaming of the works hooter at South Queensferry Distillery. Even here, where the sirens did sound, few took any notice preferring to go outside and watch the fun.

Possibly spurred on by the fact that his house had been sprayed with bullets, albeit British ones, Lord Provost Henry Steele stated that he was 'very annoyed', and that he was determined to get to the bottom of the mystery of why there had been no warning. Ten minutes after the raid had begun, Chief Constable Morren had telephoned the office of the District Civil Defence Commissioner, City Treasurer Will Darling, only to find them in complete ignorance of events. No information could be gleaned from the Regional Commissioner's office either. His official complaint was then directed at the Scottish Office who fobbed him off onto the Chief Constable of Midlothian Constabulary. The truth was that the sounding of sirens was carried out on the orders of the RAF and, without radar cover, there could be little clear knowledge of an impending raid.

At the beginning of December the Pentland Hills again reverberated to the sight and sound of Spitfires chasing a twin-engined bomber. The bomber was in fact an RAF Blenheim playing the part of Hans Storp's JU 88 for the propaganda film 'Squadron 992' which featured the Forth raid. John Dickson took the *Dayspring* to sea to re-enact his rescue of the three German aircrew. As conditions were too rough for filming off Port Seton, the unit moved across into sheltered water in the lee of Inchkeith. There they were promptly arrested by the Battery Commander who, on seeing their cameras, was convinced that they were spies!

Both Pat Gifford and George Pinkerton were awarded the DFC for their victories. Helmut Pohle was plucked from the sea off Crail by the coaster with which he had nearly collided. Shortly afterwards, he was transferred by whaler to the destroyer HMS *Jervis*, along with the body of one of his crew. Once aboard the destroyer and prior to losing consciousness, he was interrogated in German by Paymaster Lieutenant Ralph Engledue, Captain Philip Mack's secretary. He had sustained a fractured skull and facial injuries in the crash and, on coming to some days later in the naval hospital at Port Edgar, he recalls being visited one rather dull day by George Pinkerton. Years later, he described his opponent as, 'just the presentation of a nice young officer of the Royal Air Force'.

Three of Pohle's front teeth had been declined in the crash and were straightened using a clamp which was turned every second day. He had little confidence in this form of treatment, thinking, 'This is the famous Scottish thriftiness'. He still has the teeth. On 2 December 1939 Helmut Pohle left Edinburgh and was taken to the

The bodies of Kurt Seydel and August Schleicher are borne up Brunstane Road on their way to Portobello Cemetery. They were reburied after the war in the German war cemetery at Cannock Chase.

(603 SQUADRON ARCHIVES)

Tower of London before going on to No.1 POW camp at Grizedale Hall in Westmoreland.

Royal Navy casualties amounted to 16 killed and 44 wounded, mostly in HMS *Mohawk*. The Luftwaffe lost two aircraft, four aircrew killed and four taken prisoner. The first funerals took place on Friday 20 October. Youngest of the six naval casualties buried that morning at Douglas Bank cemetery near Rosyth was 18-year-old Ordinary Seaman Bernard Roebuck from Mohawk. The bodies of Kurt Seydel and August Schleicher, which had been recovered from the sea off Crail, were laid in St Philip's Church, Portobello, until their funeral later that day. The two coffins were placed on an RAF trailer and draped in Nazi flags. Thousands lined Brunstane Road and Milton Road as the cortege, which included Lord Provost Steele, Regional Commissioner Tom Johnston, Air Vice-Marshal Richard Saul, a large contingent from both the Glasgow and Edinburgh Squadrons and 603's pipe band playing *Over the Sea to Skye* made its way to Portobello cemetery.

The day after the Forth raid, 602's Operational Record Book contains the following signal received from Air Chief Marshal Sir Hugh Dowding, Commander-in-Chief Fighter Command: 'Well done, first blood to the Auxiliaries'.

One of the congratulatory telegrams received by 603 Squadron reads, 'Nice work boys, Turrnhoose uber alles!'

Chapter Three

Engaged In Treasonable Practices

'One of the most deadly blows that could be struck against Hitler and the Nazi party would be to impeach his friends in this country.'
(Willie Gallacher MP during the Munich debate in the House of Commons on 4 October 1938.)

'Yesterday was a day of black despair. Such an end to that beautiful ship, and how one wished she could have accounted for at least one good shot into the *Hood*.'
(From a letter written by a Right Club member in December 1939, on hearing of the sinking of the *Graf Spee*.)

London's Onslow Square is tree lined, elegant and exclusive. It has changed little since the morning of Thursday 23 May 1940 when two detectives kept watch on No. 24. A car drew up and the detectives moved to arrest its tall, immaculately dressed occupant. Captain Archibald Maule Ramsay, wealthy landowner, fascist and the Unionist Member of Parliament for Peebles and South Midlothian was destined to spend the next four years and four months in Brixton Prison. He was interned under the provisions of Defence Regulation 18B as one who was likely to endanger public safety and the war effort. Neville Chamberlain, chairing the previous day's War Cabinet during Churchill's absence in France, had told his colleagues that, 'Captain Maule Ramsay MP, who was the principal organiser of the Right Club, has been engaged in treasonable practices'.

Received wisdom on the Ramsay case has been that he was a lone eccentric with few friends and little influence. New evidence reveals that this was far from the true case and that sympathy, even enthusiasm, for the fascist dictators in Europe was well established at all levels within Scottish society.

In 1914, the establishment and the Church combined to inspire a crusade of medieval proportions against the evil Hun. Around 110,000 Scots died between 1914 and 1918, approximately 10 per cent of the male population between 16 and 50. Well over 90 per cent came from the ranks and, almost by definition, the working classes.

By 1919, violent revolutionary changes had occurred in both Russia and Germany, both of which led to the overthrow of many of the icons of wealth and privilege. France, Britain's major ally in the First World War, was in the grip of political instability which would continue to plague it until the end of the Second World War. In Britain, the privileged classes looked on with mounting horror as these events unfolded in Europe and unrest began to spread to this country. Scottish politics had begun to move leftwards in the years before the 1914-18 war, matters coming to a dramatic head in 1919 when tanks appeared on the streets of Glasgow in response to the so-called George Square riots.

In the 1922 General Election, greater enfranchisement meant that 42 per cent of Glasgow's electorate voted Labour and some 31 left wing MPs were elected to Parliament including the Communist, Willie Gallacher in Fife. Amid euphoric scenes following the 1922 election, the 'Red Clydesiders' had marched at the head of a large crowd to St Enoch's Station. The promise of James Maxton that the railways would, 'all belong to the people when we come back', was utter anathema and a direct challenge to the established order. Two years later Ramsay MacDonald formed his first minority Labour government.

In the event, the political pendulum swung against the new Left with the failure of both the General Strike in 1926 and the second Labour administration in 1931. The growing international political crisis, along with the disastrous economic depression, led to the formation of the National government led, successively, by Stanley Baldwin and Neville Chamberlain. Notionally a coalition government, it was in effect Conservative and, given the weakness of the Labour Party, electorally unassailable. This had the effect of pushing many towards the fringes of politics, fringes only too willing to welcome influential men and women increasingly frustrated at the threat posed to their position by a war with Germany.

The focus of attention for left and right alike in the mid-30s was not yet the new Nazi government in Germany. It was a revolt started by an obscure Spanish officer, Francisco Franco. The Spanish Civil War was a straight fight between a democratically elected left-wing government supported by an undemocratic Soviet Union, and fascist rebels led by Franco and supported by an equally undemocratic Germany. It polarised world opinion in a way that the First World War had failed to do.

Captain Archibald 'Jock' Ramsay was born in India in 1894 into one of Scotland's most distinguished families. Education at Eton and Sandhurst was followed by military service in the Second Battalion, the Coldstream Guards, one of the first units to be sent to France in August 1914. Promoted to Captain in 1915, he was severely wounded in 1916 and awarded the Military Cross for gallantry. A staff post at the War Office followed and, shortly after receiving a medical discharge in 1918, he married Ismay, the eldest daughter of Viscount Gormanston and widow of Lord Ninian Crichton-Stuart MP. In addition to the London house at Onslow Square, Ramsay owned Kellie Castle, Arbroath. From there, he was able to fulfil his passion for field sports.

In the 1920s he began a round of speaking engagements at which he denounced the evils of communism and 'international Jewry'. His set piece was entitled 'Red Wings Over Europe'. In it he sought to build up the picture of conspiracy run by Jews and communists intent on dominating Europe and, in particular, Britain. Despite, or perhaps even because of, the fact that he had been stumping the country proclaiming his views for some years, he was accepted as the Unionist candidate for the Peebles and South Midlothian constituency in 1931. He roundly defeated the sitting Labour MP, Joseph Westwood, and swept into Parliament with a secure majority. He was not a success at Westminster. The only highlight in an otherwise lacklustre career appears to have been brief service as Parliamentary Member of the Potato Marketing Board.

By 1937 Katharine, Duchess of Atholl, had been the Unionist MP for Kinross and West Perthshire for 12 years. That April she paid a short visit to Spain as a member of a delegation of women MPs. What she saw made a deep and lasting impression. She was immediately struck by the misery and suffering of refugees from Franco's

Captain Archibald Maule Ramsay.
Ramsay's apologists have maintained that he would never have involved himself in treachery. This is hard to reconcile with his willingness to use government documents he knew to be stolen in order to force Churchill out of office and bring about a negotiated peace with Germany.

(HERALD AND EVENING TIMES)

falangists and soon saw him for what he was: a ruthless fascist. Communist rebel Dolores Ibarurri, better known as 'La Passionara', impressed her but she returned to Britain adamant that the democratically elected coalition was the only legitimate government. Immediately on her return she began to raise money for refugee relief and took part in a campaign to bring the children of republican families to a place of safety in Britain.

In Perthshire a campaign against her humanitarian efforts began almost immediately. Local landowners, led by Colonel Rupert Dawson of Braco, started by sending her abusive letters. The Duchess's stand soon attracted the hostile attentions of the Scottish Tory establishment. She was forced to resign the party whip and offer herself for re-election as an independent.

Largely fought on issues of foreign policy, the campaign which followed was, even for the time, bitter. Blackshirts appeared on the streets of Auchterarder, Aberfeldy and Crieff and a veritable queue of senior Conservatives formed to speak on behalf of William Snadden, the official Conservative candidate who toed the party line towards appeasement. Prominent among these was Lord Dunglass, then the MP for North Lanark and later, as Sir Alec Douglas Home, Prime Minister in the 1960s. Scottish Chief Whip Sir James Stuart, later Viscount Stuart of Findhorn, and Ernest Brown, the Minister of Labour and a future Secretary of State for Scotland also appeared for Snadden. Lord Mansfield spoke in his support and referred to what he termed 'the oppression of the German minorities in Czechoslovakia'. He referred to Churchill as 'a public menace'.

Support for Atholl came from anti-appeasers such as Anthony Eden, Glasgow's Lord Provost Paddy Dollan, Liberal Peer Viscount Cecil, Aberdeen MP Bob Boothby and President of the Glasgow University Liberal Club John Junor. It was not enough. Snadden won the seat with a majority of 1,313 votes on a low poll. Some local landowners even resorted to the highly illegal practice of sending their tenants leaflets in support of Snadden along with pointed letters about the rent.

Prominent among those who spoke against Atholl was Captain Ramsay. When the Spanish Civil War broke out he was one of the first and most voluble opponents of the anti-Franco International Brigades of volunteers, describing them as 'the Godless'. This led to him being offered the chairmanship of the United Christian Front, an umbrella organisation of Franco supporters which counted among its membership the Earl of Home and many prominent Conservatives including Victor Cazelet, who pronounced in March 1938 that, 'Franco is the leader of our cause today'. Financial support for Franco came from many of Britain's industrial giants, such as Rio Tinto Zinc.

Oswald Mosley's British Union of Fascists had a largely working-class appeal and made little headway in Scotland where, until 1934, its principal organiser was Dr Robert Forgan, a son of the manse and the former Labour MP for West Renfrew.

One of the BUF's most ardent advocates was William Chambers-Hunter, a landowner from Udny, Aberdeenshire, who first became active in May 1937. Typical of his meetings was one which took place at the Market Stance in Aberdeen on Sunday, 3 October 1937, and was timed to coincide with a major rally in London. Clearly expecting trouble, Chambers-Hunter turned up in a van protected by wire-netting only to be surrounded by around 5,000 jeering Aberdonians. A number of people were hurt in the ensuing scuffles.

Scuffles also broke out at a similar meeting in Edinburgh's Jeffrey Street just over a week later. One witness recorded that he could see 'nothing but fists flying'. Two days later six arrests were made at a meeting organised in Parliament Square by R. A. Plathen, the fascist candidate for the St Giles ward. A running battle took place down the steps from the Mound to Princes Street and on into Frederick Street. That same month saw a German teacher in Coatbridge being heavily criticised for lecturing on the virtues of the Hitler Youth movement. Dr Heinrich Hoffman was required to cease his lectures, despite the fact that this was 'regretted' by members of the local Scout movement.

Meanwhile, Germany, rather than Spain, was becoming the focus of attention and a number of pro-Nazi groups were being formed. One of the first was the January Club set up in 1934 by, amongst others, Captain Luttman-Johnson of Luncarty near Perth. Luttman-Johnson it was who organised a rally in support of Franco in Perth during the Duchess of Atholl's election campaign. Speakers included Sir Nairne Stewart-Sandeman MP and Sir Walter Max-well-Scott MP, who referred to anti-fascist hecklers as 'scum'. Contemporary reports state that Stewart-Sandeman's speech was very pro-fascist and contained the assertion that people 'talked a lot of nonsense' about the bombing of Guernica.

Among the influential members of Luttman-Johnson's January Club were Lord William Scott, brother of the eighth Duke of Buccleuch and the Unionist MP for Roxburgh and Selkirk from 1935 to 1950. Also a member was Lord Erskine, the eldest son of the twelfth Earl of Mar and MP for Weston-Super-Mare who held the post of Assistant Government Whip in the National government in 1934. Other members included Colonel Ivan Guthrie of Guthrie and Sir Henry Fairfax-Lucy, the owner of large estates in the Borders, near Fort William, in Warwickshire and in Kenya.

Sir Adrian Baillie was the Unionist MP for Linlithgow from 1931 until he lost his seat in 1935. In 1933, one year before joining the January Club, he acted as host when Rosenberg, one of Hitler's top Jew baiters, visited Britain. Despite the fact that Rosenberg placed a wreath bedecked with a large swastika on the Cenotaph, Baillie later said that 'the anti-German spirit which has resulted from the Nazi revolution has been entirely overdone'. The wreath was thrown in the Thames by a retired army officer. Baillie served as member for Tonbridge in Kent from 1937 to 1945.

Formed in 1935 and twinned with the Deutsche-Englische Gesellschaft, the Anglo-German Fellowship was less overtly pro-Nazi than some organisations and hid its true character behind a veneer of respectability. It counted among its membership the Marquess of Clydesdale, a famous pre-war pilot and later the Duke of Hamilton. Perhaps unwisely, Clydesdale wrote to the *Times* in October 1939 stating that, 'This generation is conscious that great injustices were done to the German people in the era after the last war. There must be no repetition of that'. He continued with the curiously illogical assertion that, 'We do not grudge Germany Lebensraum, provided that Lebensraum is not made the grave of other nations'. The Earl of Airlie and Lord Arbuthnot, the Lord Lieutenant of Kincardineshire, were members of the Anglo-German fellowship, as were Guy Burgess and Kim Philby who used the organisation to establish right-wing credentials. The Earl of Glasgow, then serving on Ayrshire County Council, had been a prominent member of the pro-Mussolini British Fascisti in the 1920s and was a member along with Lord Lothian, the British Ambassador in Washington in 1939 and 1940.

A fellow pupil at Eton with Ramsay, Lord Erskine and Lord Scott was Colonel William Francis Forbes-Sempill, 19th Baron Sempill. A pioneer aviator, he had joined the Royal Flying Corps in August

1914. After the war he was instrumental in the development of the Japanese Naval Air Service which was to prove so effective against the American and British navies in the Pacific. He was also involved in the development of the Greek Air Force and had given lectures to the German Aeronautical Society in Berlin. A pillar of the establishment with estates at Craigievar and Fintray in Aberdeenshire, he was also a member of the Royal National Lifeboat Institution, the Science Museum Advisory Committee, President of the British Gliding Association and Vice-President of London Chamber of Commerce. He was also a known enthusiast for Hitler and the Nazi party.

Sir Thomas Moore joined the army in 1908, serving in France and, between 1918 and 1920, the Soviet Union where he had observed the revolution at first hand. He was twice mentioned in despatches and received various other awards including the White Eagle of Serbia. He left the army in 1925 and became the Unionist Member of Parliament for Ayr Burghs. A Fellow of the Royal Geographical Society and a Trustee of the Royal Society for the Prevention of Cruelty to Animals, he was also a Freeman of the City of London.

Following a visit to Hitler in Berlin in October 1933, Moore, an avowed admirer of the Nazis and sometime confidant of Oswald Mosley, said of Germany's new leader that 'peace and justice are the keywords of his policy'. Later, in 1935, he said that Germany had been 'rescued' by Hitler. In turn, the Fuhrer said of Moore that he was 'a man of peace, a statesman and a clear-sighted administrator of his country'. In 1938, the year of the Munich Agreement, Moore said of Germany, 'God forbid that we should fight (such) a friendly and kindly people.' He was also a member of the Anglo-German Fellowship. He remained MP for the redrawn Ayr constituency until 1964.

Not to be confused with the Anglo-German Fellowship was the *Anglo-German Review*, a glossy, high-quality publication produced by another pro-Nazi organisation called Link. Formed in 1937 under the chairmanship of Admiral Sir Barry Domvile, a former Director of Naval Intelligence, Link was little more than a mouthpiece for Goebbels, Hitler's propaganda chief who funded many of its activities. By May 1939 it had well over 4,000 active members and 31 branches which, in addition to disseminating pro-German propaganda, indulged in musical evenings, mystery tours and nature rambles. One hundred and twenty people attended the inaugural meeting of the Glasgow branch which was held in the city's Ca'doro restaurant on 24 February 1939. The reply to Domvile's address was delivered by Edward Rosslyn Mitchell, a respected Glasgow Town Councillor, solicitor and Justice of the Peace who had served as the Labour Member of Parliament for Paisley from 1924 to 1929. The first meeting of the Edinburgh branch was organised for the following night by Edinburgh University historian, Professor Charles Sarolea. *Anglo-German Review* reported that Domvile, a virulent anti-semite and fascist, was given an 'enthusiastic reception' by those present.

A member of the Governing Council of Link was distinguished Edinburgh academic and Fellow of King's College, Cambridge, Professor A. P. Laurie. Archibald Crawford KC, a leading member of the Scottish Bar for 21 years and, coincidentally, a former Parliamentary candidate for Peebles, was also a member, as was Captain Ramsay. Further names of note attached to Link include Lord Sempill, Sir Thomas Moore, Lord Lothian, Lord Fairfax of Cameron and, from south of the border, a whole string of senior military men, academics, MPs, including David Lloyd George, and industrialists, including Lord Nuffield, the Chairman of Morris Motors Ltd.

The Duke of Buccleuch paid regular visits to Hitler, whom he openly admired. General Sir Ian Hamilton, Scotland's most famous old soldier and the former British Commander-in-Chief at Gallipoli, was also visiting the Fuhrer secretly under the cover of British Legion visits to Europe. Another distinguished Scottish soldier was Lieutenant-Colonel Graham Seton Hutchison MC DSO. A violent anti-semite and pro-fascist, in 1933 he had been behind the formation of the National Workers Party of Great Britain, an outfit closely modelled on the German Nazi party. A member of the British Legion and the first chairman of the Old Contemptible Association, he once told a gathering of ex-servicemen: 'We will not permit the cream of the youth of our country, and of the Empire, to be sent again to the shambles to line the pockets of the Jews and their puppets.' He worked for the Nazis as a publicist and went so far as to inform on anti-Nazis to Rosenberg and Hitler. The fate of these unfortunates is not recorded.

It was of course inconceivable that all this at least potentially subversive activity could be undertaken without coming under the scrutiny of the Security Service or, as it is otherwise known, MI5. Led by Brigadier 'Jasper' Harker, MI5's B Division was responsible for counter-espionage and anti-subversion. One of Harker's most talented officers was Maxwell Knight, an enigmatic former naval officer and teacher, who had been recruited in 1924. A keen amateur naturalist and jazz musician, he also wrote dreadful pulp fiction and, as a close friend of Dennis Wheatley, dabbled in the occult.

In 1937 Knight, or 'M' as he liked to be known, set up his own section, B5b, in Dolphin Square, an ugly development on London's Embankment. From Flat 308, Hood House, Knight ran a network of agents infiltrated into both communist and fascist groups. In the fervid political atmosphere of the late 1930s, Knight's secretive organisation flourished and expanded into a further flat next door in Collingwood House.

Among the first organisations to attract Knight's attention in 1937 was the Nordic League, a first attempt by Ramsay and others including the former Scottish Labour MP, Dr Robert Forgan, to bring together all the various fascist organisations under one collective head. In October 1939, in a report entitled 'The Fascist Movement in this Country at the Present Time', Knight informed the Home Secretary, Sam Hoare, that the Nordic League was advocating violence. He continued that 'we know from an absolutely reliable source that the League has been in touch with the Nazi authorities in Germany'. A letter from Jasper Harker to Sir Edward Holderness, Permanent Under Secretary at the Home Office reads;

SECRET   BOX No. 500
                             PARLIAMENT STREET B.O.
                                   LONDON S.W.1.

                                  13th October, 1939.

Dear Holderness,

I feel that it should be brought to your notice that at a meeting of the Nordic League held on Monday, October 8th, the question of communicating with Germany was discussed. It was suggested that Ireland should be utilised for this purpose as the nearest neutral country.

Yours sincerely,

Allan Harker

Sir Samuel Chapman, Unionist MP for Edinburgh South and a member of the Right Club. Chapman was an active supporter of the Perth and Perthshire POW Fund.

It has been suggested that Right Club members were unaware of the true nature of the organisation they had joined. This argument carries little weight as Captain Ramsay had been loudly proclaiming his pro-fascist, anti-Semitic views for years before its formation. In addition, Right Club meetings were enlivened by songs composed by Ramsay, one of which was entitled Land of dope and Jewry, *and was sung to the tune of* Land of Hope and Glory. *Its last verse reads:*

Longer still and longer
Is the rope they get
But, by the God of Battles
T'will serve to hang them yet.

This was said to have been composed on the day Britain declared war on Germany.

(HERALD AND EVENING TIMES)

According to a Special Branch report prepared for the Home Office on 23 May 1940, 'it has been possible to secure reliable reports of the proceedings at these "closed" meetings of the League; the themes of the speeches made thereat are, without exception, anti-semitism of a very virulent kind and a eulogy of Nazism'. Among the enthusiastically received speakers was Captain Ramsay who ended one anti-semitic diatribe with the chilling assertion that, 'The British people should rid themselves of this menace (the Jews), and if one method did not work, another should be tried . . . any means, whatever they were, would be used if necessary'. In regular attendance was Takayuki Iguchi, a Japanese intelligence service officer posing as a journalist.

The Nordic League was however too public an organisation for most of Ramsay's influential friends. At the beginning of 1939 he began the formation of the secret society which would gain him lasting fame and lead to his downfall; the Right Club.

In his report on fascist groups in Britain, Knight refers to the Right Club as having been formed in 1939 with the object of amalgamating and strengthening various extreme right wing and pro-fascist movements. He continues, 'From two independent sources we learn that the activity of the Right Club is centred principally upon the contacting of sympathisers, especially among officers in the armed forces, and the spreading by personal talks of the club's ideals. There is talk of a military coup, but there seems to be lack of agreement among members on the question of leadership.'

As the war clouds gathered over Europe, Ramsay was attracting members including Sir Samuel Chapman, since 1922 the Unionist MP for Edinburgh South. A prominent businessman and JP, Chapman was also a member of the Perthshire Education Authority and Chairman of the Perth Academy Management Committee.

Richard Stokes sat on the board of Scottish companies and was the Labour MP for Ipswich. Earlier he had stood unsuccessfully for the Glasgow Central constituency. A member of the Right Club, following the debacle at Dunkirk in 1940, he was one of a number of MPs advocating a negotiated peace with Germany. After the war, he became Minister of Works and a Privy Counsellor.

Colonel Sir Harold Mitchell was chairman of the Alloa Coal Company and Alloa Glassworks, he was also president of two Canadian mining companies and a director of the London and North Eastern Railway Company. A wealthy sportsman who was

joint Master of the Lauderdale Foxhounds and who had represented Britain in international ski-ing competitions, he owned
Tulliallan Castle at Kincardine-on-Forth along with a considerable
estate in Jamaica and a third home in Austria. The Conservative
member for Clackmannan and East Stirlingshire from 1929 to
1931, he had since represented the safe seat of Brentford and
Chiswick. He remained a JP and Deputy Lieutenant of the County
of Clackmannan and was a Right Club member.

Lieutenant-Colonel Charles Kerr DSO MC became the National
Liberal member for Montrose Burghs in 1932. A Lord Commissioner of the Treasury and Chief Whip of the National Liberal Party,
he was a stockbroker by profession. He too joined Ramsay's
organisation, as did John Hamilton McKie, a landowner from
Castle Douglas, who had first stood as a Unionist candidate for the
Edinburgh Central constituency in 1929. In 1931 he was successful
in his bid for the Galloway constituency.

From industry Ramsay was able to recruit Sir Alexander Walker,
the Chairman of Johnny Walker Distillers. Others who joined
included Lord Carnegie, later Earl Southesk who married Princess
Maud, Queen Victoria's grand-daughter, and the Marquis of Graham, later the Duke of Montrose, who was destined to be Minister
of Defence in Ian Smith's breakaway government in Rhodesia. Lord
Sempill was a member as was the Earl of Galloway. Randolph
Algernon Ronald Stewart, the 12th Earl of Galloway was born in
1892 and, after Harrow and war service during which he had been
taken prisoner, he succeeded to the title in 1920. Lord Lieutenant
of Kirkcudbrightshire since 1932, he owned around 69,000 acres.

One of the first to join was William Joyce, the renegade Irish-
American soon to be better known as Lord Haw Haw. Other
notable members drawn from south of the border include a number
of MPs, Baron Redesdale the father of the Mitford sisters, and the
Fifth Duke of Wellington.

With the start of the war, six months after the formation of the
Right Club, most pro-fascist organisations closed down or collapsed. Many of the leading members of the Nordic League were
rounded up as a result of Knight's report in October 1939.

The Right Club, on the other hand, was a secret society and simply
went underground where it continued to flourish unaware that it
had already been infiltrated by Max Knight's agents. Knight had a
considerable talent for running female agents and the first to

infiltrate the Right Club was Marjorie Mackie, described by one of her colleagues as a cosy middle-aged woman who reminded her of Miss Marple. She was followed by a young Belgian girl, Helene de Munck, and a former secretary at the Elizabeth Arden cosmetics firm, Joan Miller.

Ramsay's London home at Onslow Square was placed under Special Branch surveillance and the telephone tapped, though this revealed little other than that the cook was systematically robbing her employers of sugar. Other prominent Right Club members were being watched and their mail read by MI5's Letters Interception Unit.

Meetings of the Right Club Inner Circle were held above a tearoom operated by a White Russian emigr family, the Wolkoffs, in Harrington Road, South Kensington, a short distance from the Ramsay home in Onslow Square. Admiral Wolkoff had been the Russian Naval Attach in London at the time of the Russian Revolution, an event which he considered to be the result of a Jewish-Bolshevik conspiracy. A bitter man, much reduced in circumstances, he had bred into his daughter, Anna, a violent hatred of Jews and communists. At some point late in 1938 or early in 1939, Anna Wolkoff was introduced to Captain Ramsay. Within weeks she was describing herself as his political secretary and, with zealous fanaticism, oragnising anti-semitic and anti-war campaigns on behalf of the Right Club. These included booing when Churchill appeared on cinema newsreels and the notorious 'sticky-back' campaign conducted in the blackout following the outbreak of war. One such sticky-back was worded thus:

PJ   PJ
Last time it was
KITCHENER WANTS YOU!

This time the JEW
HORE BELISHA WANTS YOU!

The House of Rothschild WANTS YOU!

The Jewish Board of Deputies
WANTS YOU!

Lucifer WANTS YOU in a Jewish war of
Revenge on Germany

WARS ARE THE JEWS HARVEST.
PJ   PJ

(The initials PJ stand for 'Perish Judah', a greeting reserved for each other by Right Club members.)

On the face of it, these efforts at subversion by the Right Club appear clumsy, puerile, even ludicrous. They were, however, being conducted when the public was not as politically sophisticated as it became during and after the war. At a time when public morale was seen as all important to the war effort, they were taken very seriously indeed by both the government and the Security Service.

By the spring of 1940, Knight felt that Joan Miller had gained the confidence of Right Club members, in particular Ismay Ramsay. It was arranged that Miller should invite Mrs Ramsay to afternoon tea in an MI5 officer's flat which had been specially bugged for the occasion. It was hoped that, suitably encouraged by Miller, she would offer evidence which would incriminate herself and others.

The day in question turned out to be particularly warm and it was discovered that, with the windows open to let in fresh air, traffic noise drowned out the hidden microphones. When Ismay Ramsay arrived the windows were firmly shut and the room was uncomfortably warm. In response to a request to open the window, Miller, thinking on her feet, replied that the cat might jump onto the window sill and fall to the street below. There was, of course, no cat.

Both women were ill-at-ease and Ismay Ramsay gave nothing incriminating away. When she had gone, two Special Branch officers, having spent the afternoon inside a cupboard ready to record any damning evidence, fell out into the room drenched in sweat. Joan Miller revealed much about her own personality when, by way of an apology, she gave Special Branch a pin-up photograph of herself.

A decisive breakthrough in the investigation had occurred some weeks earlier when Anna Wolkoff had taken a new acquaintance, a code clerk at the American embassy by the name of Tyler Kent, to see Captain Ramsay at his London home. Kent, who professed to be strongly against any American involvement in the war, was already under observation by MI5 after being seen in the company of Ludwig Matthias, a naturalised Swede of German origin. Matthias was suspected by the Swedes of being both a German agent and a double agent on behalf of Soviet intelligence, a fact they had communicated to MI5.

It was soon discovered that Kent was stealing copies of telegrams between Roosevelt and Churchill, then still First Lord of the Admiralty. These he was showing to Ramsay who believed, wrongly, that the correspondence was being carried on without the knowledge of Prime Minister Neville Chamberlain. Ramsay was convinced that, by exposing what he believed was a plot on the part of Churchill, he could force a negotiated end to the war.

MI5 and Special Branch began their swoop on the morning of Monday, 20 May 1940. First to be arrested was Anna Wolkoff, followed two hours later by Tyler Kent who was surprised in bed with his mistress. Dozens of other arrests, including those of Ramsay and other leading Right Club members, followed over the next few days. Among those picked up was Captain Luttman Johnson, news of whose arrest appeared in the *Dundee Courier*.

Even now, more than half a century later, the names of most of those arrested are shrouded in secrecy. Generally, it was the small-fry who were interned. Ramsay, for example, was the only MP kept in custody. Quite simply, to have thrown all those involved into jail would have caused a monumental scandal at a time when the country could least afford it. The Duke of Westminster was warned to keep quiet, as was the Marquis of Tavistock, who was known to have been in contact with German Foreign Minister Ribbentrop as late as January 1940. More sensitive were the cases of George Steward, Chamberlain's Press Officer, and Deputy Foreign Secretary R. A. Butler, both of whom had been in contact with German emissaries since the outbreak of war. FBI surveillance showed that the Duchess of Windsor continued to correspond with Ribbentrop until 1941. Both she and her husband were indiscreet and anti-war, and were kept under close MI6 surveillence.

Occasionally, the matter did resurface in the House of Commons, notably in July 1941 when Liberal MP Geoffrey Mander asked Home Secretary Herbert Morrison to publish the names on the Right Club membership list which had been found in Tyler Kent's flat. As Morrison's own file notes show, this was impossible, not least because some of those named were still being watched by MI5.

Not a few MPs must have squirmed with embarrassment when Labour maverick Manny Shinwell, clearly intent on making mischief, intervened to ask for an assurance that no honourable members were in the Right Club. Morrison could only give an evasive reply.

It would have been reasonable to assume that, given the demands of wartime, pro-fascist movements would have disappeared, or at least gone underground, for the duration. In 1943, however, Herbert Morrison began to receive a stream of complaints about *Vanguard*, a publication produced in Glasgow by an organisation calling itself the British Protestant League. Typical of the articles it contained were those headlined, 'SENSATIONAL - BRITISH BOMB GERMAN CHURCHES', and, 'JEWISH ORIGINS OF THE RED FLAG'.

Enquiries by B4a section of MI5 revealed that *Vanguard* was largely the work of Alexander Ratcliffe of Endrick Drive, Bearsden, a former Edinburgh tram driver and Glasgow town councillor with known pro-fascist leanings. In addition to producing *Vanguard*, Ratcliffe's organisation held well-attended quasi-religious meetings on Sunday nights in the Central Halls, Bath Street, Glasgow.

Copies of *Vanguard* intercepted in Scotland by the Postal and Telegraph Censorship Service were passed to the B4a case officer, Roger Hollis. He ordered Special Branch detectives in Glasgow to interview Ratcliffe. It was hoped that a visit from the police would frighten him into ceasing his activities, thus avoiding the need for his internment.

In fact, mail interception later revealed that Ratcliffe was in touch with the newly resurgent British National Party in London, and had offered them copies of his pamphlet entitled 'The Truth about the Jews'.

Far more worrying for Morrison and Hollis was the report by the Glasgow detectives which stated that, whilst only 2,000 copies of each edition of *Vanguard* were being printed, demand was such that 100,000 copies could have been sold every month.

Chapter Four

Dawn Patrol From Turnhouse

'Och its you Mr Johnstone . . . the sirens went off and we thocht you was a German!'

It was just before midday on Sunday, 3 September 1939. Flight-Lieutenant Sandy Johnstone and Squadron Leader Douglas Farquhar of 602 (City of Glasgow) Squadron had just landed at Grangemouth aerodrome after an unpleasantly bumpy flight in thundery weather from Abbotsinch, west of Glasgow. They had taken off immediately on hearing Neville Chamberlain inform the nation that it was at war with Germany, and were on a mission to inspect the squadron's planned wartime base. Their flight, along with one by some aircraft off the Dutch coast, had caused the sirens to be sounded over much of central Scotland at 1120 hours, just as the Prime Minister ended his broadcast.

The first enemy attack of the war took place in the North Sea on 26 September 1939 when Heinkel 111 and Junkers 88 bombers attempted to bomb ships of the Home Fleet. Just after 1100 hours the following day two sections of 603 (City of Edinburgh) Squadron were ordered to a patrol line five miles east of May Island, there to assist the destroyer *Valorous* and the sloop *Hastings*, which had come under attack. To their discomfiture, the Edinburgh pilots were subjected to a barrage of anti-aircraft fire from the destroyer, which was clearly operating on the shoot first and ask questions later principle.

Many ignored the warning which was sounded over Edinburgh at 1130 hours on Friday 20 October, others could not find space in overcrowded shelters at West Princes Street Gardens. Postmen carried on with deliveries. One pedestrian took shelter in first a Catholic church, then a Presbyterian one, and finally a Co-op store as three separate alerts were sounded. A correspondent in the *Scotsman* was moved to ask if those in Edinburgh who had been 'clamouring for siren warnings are now satisfied that they are getting their money's worth?'

At Mackie's Rooms in Princes Street a number of guests did not arrive for a National Temperance League lunch. Banks emptied their tills and, at Dalkeith High School pupils were taken from the second floor to the basement. The first-aid post at the Knox Institute in Haddington reported ready for duty at 1131 hours. Dunfermline streets had to be cleared of the curious by wardens and, in Kirkcaldy, it was reported that the locals 'took the sirens calmly'. A number of false alarms followed. One major alert was declared when 27 enemy aircraft were detected approaching from the north. These turned out to be an entirely friendly flight of geese.

Following their blooding on 16 October (see Chapter 2), 603 were soon back in action. At 1435 hours on 22 October Red Section, led by Pat Gifford, were ordered up from Turnhouse to intercept two enemy aircraft attacking a convoy off St Abbs Head. These aircraft were Heinkel 111s of 1(F)/122, a long-range reconnaissance unit, which had been plotted flying south from Dundee. Gifford's section brought one down seven miles offshore whereupon three of its crew were seen taking to their dinghy. Unteroffizier Endorf was already dead when the aircraft hit the water and his body was not found. After refuelling, the Spitfires returned to the scene where they succeeded in guiding the destroyer HMS *Gurkha* to pick up the survivors. Both Colin Robertson's and 'Black' Morton's Spitfires had been damaged by return fire.

At Drone Hill radar station, RAF personnel were surprised to receive a telephone call, on what was supposed to be a high security line, from a *Daily Herald* reporter wanting information on the action.

Drone Hill first detected plot X40 at 0836 hours on Saturday, October 28. It was tracked north-west and crossed the coast near Earlsferry before going west to the Firth of Clyde where the crew had been ordered to photograph shipping. Due to cloud cover this was not possible and it returned east from Helensburgh, following the line of the Forth and Clyde Canal to Falkirk, thence to Aberdour where it came under fire from vessels anchored in the river.

It was estimated that around 300 rounds had hit the Heinkel 111 (1H+JA) of KG 26 before it crashed on Kidlaw Hill near Humbie. The crest of KG 26 was a Lion Rampant in a green heraldic shield under the motto 'Vestigium Leonis'. Lieutenant Dangerfield, Intelligence Officer of the 3rd Anti-Aircraft Division, considered the Lion Rampant a wholly inappropriate emblem for a Luftwaffe unit. He took comfort from the fact that the literal translation of the biological term 'vestigium' is an organ which has lost any use it once possessed.

(603 SQUADRON ARCHIVES)

At 0916 hours Red Section of 603 Squadron were scrambled to look for the raider near Helensburgh. Five minutes later, Red Section, 602 Squadron, were ordered off from Drem to patrol over the Firth of Forth. Flying Officer Archie McKellar, Red Leader, first saw anti-aircraft shells bursting round the enemy bomber south of Inchkeith.

Meanwhile, a round from one of the ships below had burst close alongside the Heinkel, riddling it with splinters and damaging the port engine. The navigator and commander of the bomber, Leutnant Rolf Neihoff, ordered his pilot, Unteroffizier Kurt Lehmkuhl, to dive into the security of cloud.

McKellar led his section into attack. After his second firing pass, he clearly saw that the bomber's port engine was out of action and smoking. He also reported that his victim was about to make a forced landing. At that moment three more Spitfires came streaking in from the west. Red Section of 603 Squadron had raced back eastwards from their wild-goose chase to Helensburgh.

The interior of the bomber was reduced to a shambles. Both the wireless operator/gunner Bruno Reimann and the flight engineer/gunner Gottleib Kowalke had been shot dead. As he tried to keep control long enough to crash land, Kurt Lehmkuhl suffered agonising back wounds from one of 603's aircraft.

At 1022 hours, observers on the ground saw the bomber being chased over Prestonpans and Tranent. That afternoon, the local football club proudly showed off a bullet hole in the window of their bus. The fight continued over Colstoun and Gifford before the bomber turned back to crash land on the gentler slopes near Humbie village. An eyewitness told the BBC he had heard 'a noise like the hurling of a barrow . . . it went on and came nearer and nearer, and then I knew it was gunfire'. He continued that he had seen a big black bomber being chased by four fighters which 'were circling round and rattling bullets into the German as hard as they could do it'.

Doctor Richard Graham-Millar, who was spending the weekend with his parents at nearby Longnewton Farm, was one of the first to reach the downed bomber. Neihoff had managed to extricate his pilot from the wreck and, using the first-aid kit from the Heinkel, Graham-Miller dressed Lehmkuhl's wounds.

Police from Haddington soon arrived on the scene and Neihoff surrendered himself to them, shaking hands with his pilot before being led away. Lehmkuhl was carried down the hill on a farm gate as were the bodies of Reimann and Kowalke, thence by ambulance to Edinburgh Castle. Neihoff was taken to Edinburgh Castle after being entertained to lunch by army officers. He expressed his surprise that, contrary to rumour in Germany, there was plenty of food to be had in Scotland. Only when he reached the Tower of London was it discovered that he had sustained a broken back.

The following week a reporter shown a spent machine-gun bullet from the Heinkel, saw in it what he described as a fracture. This, he gleefully informed readers of the Edinburgh *Evening News*, was evidence of inferior quality.

Enemy operations against the River Forth were intended to close it to shipping by dropping both magnetic and acoustic mines. At 0917 hours on 21 October 1939 the new 10,500-ton cruiser, HMS *Belfast*, sailed from Rosyth along with HMS *Southampton*. Escorted by the destroyer HMS *Afridi* they were to undertake a practice shoot off May Island. At 1058 hours, *Belfast* was between Inchkeith and May

As the first enemy aircraft to crash on British soil, the Humbie Heinkel was of considerable interest to intelligence officers. One engine was removed for examination by Rolls-Royce and the workmanship on the aircraft was described as 'first rate'. Among the contents carefully examined by the RAF were two packets of chocolate wafers, tins of chocolate powder and bully beef, three bags of hard square biscuits which were likened to dog biscuits, a slice of German sausage and a sandwich of good but stale white bread. All of this was despatched to London that night along with various notebooks which contained details of British ships.

(603 SQUADRON ARCHIVES)

Island when, according to one eyewitness, she was 'literally lifted out of the water' by the force of an explosion.

A magnetic mine had exploded under the port side of A boiler room causing 21 casualties one of whom, Rating S. Stanton, died later of head injuries. Immediate preparations were made to abandon ship. By 1120 hours the tugs *Krooman* and *Buchanan* had reached her, however she was able to make three knots under her own steam and was secured in dry dock at Rosyth at 1649 hours.

Damage to the *Belfast* included extensive flooding and turbines blown off their mountings as the ship had broken her back. As Admiral Ramsay, the Flag Officer Rosyth, put it in his war diary,

'Another lucky day for the enemy. *Belfast* is one of our latest six-inch cruisers and will be out of action for a considerable period.' Serious consideration was given to scrapping her and she did not rejoin the fleet until late 1942 after having been almost completely rebuilt at Davenport.

At 1100 hours on Tuesday, 12 December 1939, residents of North Berwick watched as Blue Section, 602 Squadron, engaged a Heinkel 111 overhead. Shortly afterwards, Spitfires of Green Section, 72 Squadron from Leuchars and Blue Section, 603 Squadron, engaged two groups of enemy aircraft over Fife. Though neither squadron made a positive claim, an Icelandic ship reported picking up a distress call at 1335 hours from an enemy aircraft which had crashed 40 miles out to sea. Coastal Command Hudsons mounted an unsuccessful search for survivors. That night the Germans confirmed that one of their aircraft was missing.

During the following day there was considerable enemy activity off the east coast. A trawler was reported sunk. On Sunday, 17 December, the Granton trawler *Compagnus* was attacked. Crew member J. Swan of Leith was killed and the cook seriously injured. The next day brought news that another Granton trawler, the *Isabella Greig*, had sunk after being bombed and strafed. Her crew, two of whom had bullet wounds, were picked up by another trawler, the *Eileen Wray*, which was also machine-gunned. The Aberdeen boat *Craigielea* was attacked at the same time and two of her crew injured. Another Granton trawler, the *River Earn*, was attacked and sunk less than 24 hours later by two enemy aircraft. Earlier, she had picked up three survivors from a Dutch steamer but they, and the trawlermen, were reported safe after 36 hours in a lifeboat.

The winter of 1939-40 was particularly severe and operations by both the RAF and Luftwaffe were necessarily restricted by blizzards and high winds. For the ground crews, that winter was a nightmare of frozen hands. On really cold days, the Spitfires' Merlin engines had to be started up every ten minutes to keep the oil from freezing. For the pilots, landing a high-performance fighter on an airfield which was really only a sodden marsh covered with a thin sheet of ice, was a hazardous experience.

Throughout that awful winter the Luftwaffe crews continued to demonstrate their courage and tenacity by flying in dreadful conditions. Using slow, draughty, often obsolete aircraft on missions which took them over nearly 500 miles of open North Sea they would suddenly appear out of thick cloud over the gale-lashed convoy lane. In addition, these courageous crews were operating against a defended coastline, in small numbers and without any fighter escort.

The weather was at least partly responsible for a tragic incident in the late afternoon of Thursday, 21 December 1939. 602 Squadron were scrambled from Drem after a raid of 12 or more bandits was detected approaching Dunbar from the east. As they shot off into the gathering gloom, a report came in to Air Operations Headquarters at Donibristle that the Naval Boom Defence Vessel *Bayonet* had just been mined less than a mile off Leith Docks. The Sector Controller at Turnhouse was successful in vectoring the Spitfires onto their quarry and Dunlop Urie led A Flight in to attack what appeared to be a formation of Dorniers.

The last thing Pilot Officer Hector McLean, flying as Red Two, heard before his TR/9 H/F radio became jammed, was Dunlop Urie's 'Tally Ho'. Sandy Johnstone, who also noted that his radio was overwhelmed by excited pilots, was leading B Flight. He came on the scene in time to see Red Section of A Flight attacking 'what appeared in bad visibility to be a Dornier'. He saw another aircraft going west about one mile north of North Berwick and ordered his section in to attack, only for another 'enemy' aircraft to rear up in front of him. He was horrified to see that it carried RAF roundels. Moments earlier, Hector McLean had seen a clear silhouette of one of the bombers, identified it as a Hampden, and did not attack.

The action was immediately broken off but not before two of the Hampden bombers from 44 Squadron had been shot down. The first crashed in the sea off North Berwick at around 1530. Two of the crew were slightly injured and all four were taken to Edmington Hospital for a check-up. The second Hampden came down in the sea off Hummel Point at Gullane. One of its crew, Leading Aircraftsman Gibbin, was drowned. The three survivors were taken to Cockenzie Police Station before being delivered to Drem.

The case of mistaken identity continued as the remaining Hampdens began landing at Drem. On seeing twin-engined bombers roar overhead, many of the ground crew were convinced a raid was in progress and dived into trench shelters only to find them half full of water.

A very tense and frosty atmosphere prevailed in the mess that evening and, during the following morning, a Court of Inquiry was convened. 602 were absolved of any blame when it was discovered that the Hampdens, which were returning from a North Sea sweep, were miles off their planned course. In addition, friendly twin-engined aircraft, which could be mistaken for 'bandits', were required to fly with their undercarriage down in defended areas; a measure designed to avoid precisely the sort of incident which had occurred and one they had failed to observe.

602 Squadron personnel were much relieved to see the Hampdens taxi out and take off for their home base at Waddington. Their relief changed to astonishment when hundreds of toilet rolls rained down about the buildings, a parting gift from 44 Squadron. The Station Commander at Drem, Group Captain Charles Keary, had been dismayed when his quiet training airfield had been turned into an operational fighter base on 24-hour readiness. To add insult to injury the Squadron visited on him was the 'long-haired amateurs' of 602. His demeanour was not improved by sight of his feifdom covered with RAF issue 'bumf' and he exacted his revenge by ordering 602's pilots to clear up the mess.

The previous morning, while the Court of Inquiry was taking evidence, the Hurricanes of 111 Squadron were ordered up along with Red Section of 602 to intercept an unidentified contact 15 miles east of May Island. Again Dunlop Urie led his section in to attack and this time there was no mistake. Although, owing to cloud, they could make no positive claim, naval units in the area later reported that one enemy aircraft had indeed been brought down. No doubt with the previous day's debacle in mind, in his combat report Hector McLean admitted to some concern over Pilot Officer 'Fumff' Strong's identification of the 'bogey' as a hostile aircraft.

After a short lull, raids began again on 9 January. Eight attacks mounted on convoys between Aberdeen and Cromer included one at St Abbs Head. 602 Squadron were up in response along with 111 Squadron from Turnhouse and 64 Squadron from Leuchars but no interceptions were made due to the appalling conditions.

From 9 January standing patrols were mounted up to 20 miles offshore over the convoy lane. Four days later a 602 Squadron patrol led by Marcus Robinson were joined by a section of 111 Squadron in shooting down Heinkel 111 F6+LH of 1(F)/122 which they had intercepted off Fife Ness. Rather cheekily, having been picked up from his dinghy, Leutnant Kahle sent a message to congratulate 602 on their shooting. Hector McLean was not impressed. He was lucky to be alive after return fire had struck his armoured windscreen.

Leutnant Kahle is reputed to have told his interrogators at Leuchars that Luftwaffe aircrews had nicknamed the Firth of Forth 'Suicide Corner'. Little wonder when one considers that his bomber had been attacked by four Spitfires and three Hurricanes.

At 1240 hours on 9 February, coastguards at North Berwick enjoyed a grandstand view as a Heinkel 111 unloaded its bombs in the sea and passed overhead. Escorted over the coast by five Spitfires, it crash-landed in a field at Rhodes Farm, south of the

The Heinkel 111 brought down by Squadron-Leader Douglas Farquhar at Rhodes Farm, North Berwick, at 1240 hours on 9 February 1940.
Clearly expecting trouble, Lieutenant-Colonel H. E. Smith sent a guard from 165 OCTU at North Berwick consisting of one officer and twelve other ranks equipped with emergency rations and 50 rounds per man. They arrived to find that local police had taken the three unwounded Germans prisoner.
The woman second from the right has obviously stood in something rural.
(SCOTSMAN NEWSPAPERS LTD)

town. Raid 36 had been plotted flying south from the Leuchars direction and had been intercepted by Red Section, 602 Squadron. His guns now harmonised for 200 yards, Douglas Farquhar fired only 625 rounds and the bomber made for the coast with its port engine streaming smoke and its rear gunner dying from a bullet wound in the lung.

On 21 February three trawlers, the *Rapatiko*, *Star of the Isles* and *Star of the East*, arrived in Leith having been damaged in an air attack.

On Thursday, 22 February 1940, Douglas Farquhar included Flying Officer George Proudman with his experimental, cannon-armed machine in A flight when it was scrambled to intercept an unidentified aircraft approaching the coast. Yellow Section, led by Sandy Johnstone, were sent to patrol the Fife coast. Red, led by Farquhar, was vectored onto a Heinkel 111 near St Abbs Head. Farquhar's attack caused the bomber's port engine to explode. Proudman followed and, inevitably, his temperamental cannons jammed after firing only 64 rounds. Lieutenant J. G. Watt watched from Drone Hill as Farquhar followed the Heinkel over the coast to Dowlaw, north of Coldingham, where it made a forced landing at 1244 hours.

The German crew were extricating themselves and their injured gunner when, to their astonishment, a Spitfire approached with its undercarriage down and attempted to land nearby. Bouncing down a steep hill it hit a patch of soft ground, dug its nose in and flipped over onto its back. Despite being intent on the destruction of their bomber, Feldwebel Sprigath, one of the German crew, ran down the hill and extricated Douglas Farquhar who was hanging upside-down in the crashed Spitfire, his nose only inches from the ground.

As soldiers appeared over the crest of a nearby hill, the intrepid Squadron Leader found himself being menaced by three distinctly unfriendly Germans brandishing Lugers. Diplomatically, he suggested to them that it might be better if they surrendered to him as the reaction of the military to the sight of armed Germans on a Scottish hillside could not be predicted.

When the soldiers arrived Farquhar had the three Lugers hidden in his flying overalls only to find that the elderly NCO in charge believed him to be one of the enemy. The situation was only resolved by the Germans pointing out the crashed Spitfire at the foot of the hill and Farquhar producing an income tax demand from his pocket.

Farquhar had in fact landed in an attempt to stop the German crew from setting fire to their aircraft as he hoped it would provide

'A' Flight of 603 Squadron early in 1940. Standing, from left: Sergeant J. R. Caister, Flying Officer Ian Ritchie, Flying Officer James 'Black' Morton, Pilot Officer George 'Sheep' Gilroy, Pilot Officer A. Barton, Warrant Officer J. Dalziel.

Seated, from left: Flying Officer J. G. E. Haig, Flight Lieutenant George Denholm, Squadron-Leader E. H. Stevens, Flying Officer Ken Macdonald, Flying Officer Alen Wallace.

The squadron went south to RAF Hornchurch in August 1940. During the Battle of Britain 'Black' Morton was shot down and badly burned. On 28 August 1940 Ian Ritchie returned to Hornchurch having been wounded in combat with ME109s off Dover. Flight-Lieutenant Cunningham and Pilot Officer Don Macdonald, Ken Macdonald's brother, were killed. Pilot Officer Benson failed to return from combat later that evening.

Ken Macdonald was killed when his Spitfire crashed near Gillingham after being bounced by ME109s at 1020 hours on 28 September. Shortly afterwards, the Macdonald brothers' mother died of a broken heart.

(603 SQUADRON ARCHIVES)

valuable evidence of the effect of cannon fire. He was disappointed to find that none of Proudman's short burst had struck home, especially as his own Spitfire was a complete write-off.

The *Royal Archer*, on passage from London to Leith, struck a mine and sank five miles south-east of Kirkcaldy that Friday. At 1305 hours on Monday, 27 February, however, 609 (West Riding) Squadron shot down an HE 111 which was attacking a convoy eight miles off St Abbs Head. The four crew were picked up and taken to Dundee by trawler. On the night of 14 March, 40 small incendiaries were dropped near Peebles and, early on 8 April, a number of high explosive bombs were jettisoned on farmland near Eddleston. A mixed load of incendiaries and high explosive bombs fell around Dalmeny House on 26 April but by then, the focus of operations had moved to Norway and Denmark.

At 2330 on 25 June around 15 KG 26 Heinkels were detected approaching the Forth area from their new base at Stavanger. The first bomb exploded between Dundonald Pits and Auchterderran in Fife at 0020 hours. A group of five Heinkels, seen crossing the coast at North Berwick at 0035 hours, scattered bombs over the Broxburn and Livingston area. First to fall were five high explosive bombs and 30 incendiaries which came down across the Lanark Road at Glenpark Estate, Balerno. Bombs then fell at Humbie and Kirknewton, at East Calder Station where a small fire was started by incendiaries, and at Mid Calder. At Howden Farm, Livingston, a woman and her son were killed when their farmhouse received a direct hit. At Broxburn a house, school and shop suffered slight damage and an incendiary fell into the Candle Works, fortunately failing to ignite. The last bombs fell at Oatridge Farm, Ecclesmachan.

One of the raiders was caught in the beam of searchlights and intercepted by Flight-Lieutenant Ken MacDonald of 603 Squadron at 0105 hours. He attacked and it went into a spiral dive emitting flame and smoke before crashing into the Forth between Grangemouth and Crombie. This was only the second successful night interception by a Spitfire. Credit for the first goes to 616 (County of Yorkshire) Squadron, who had brought down a Heinkel 111 of 3/KG4 off Withernsea around 40 minutes earlier.

At least one Heinkel broke away from the main formation and was plotted at 0120 hours over Beith in Ayrshire before passing over Ardeer, where its intended target, the ICI works, was obscured by

602 Squadron outside the Watch Office at Drem in October 1940. From left: Flying Officer Finlay Boyd, Flight-Lieutenant George Pinkerton, Flight Lieutenant Sandy Johnstone, Flying Officer Paul Webb, Flying Officer Alastair Grant, Pilot Officer Nigel Graeme.
(602 SQUADRON ARCHIVES)

cloud. Moving north-west, it passed south of Glasgow and crossed back to the Forth. The bomber was seen passing over Falkirk before being engaged by Squadron Leader George Denholm and Pilot Officer Dudley Stewart-Clark in a 603 Squadron Spitfire. Stewart-Clark reported moving out of range when the bomber was fired on by the anti-aircraft battery at West Pilton in Edinburgh. Seriously damaged by the first AA rounds, it jettisoned five bombs and 100 incendiaries east of Craigmillar Castle Road.

Squadron Leader George Pinkerton and Sandy Johnstone had been ordered up on patrol over Drem at 0125 hours. At 0155 they could see anti-aircraft fire in the Edinburgh direction and could hear the 603 Squadron call sign, 'Viken'. Suddenly, the bomber was picked up in searchlights with, as Johnstone confirmed, smoke coming from its starboard engine. Stewart-Clark watched as Johnstone took up the chase. In his combat report Johnstone describes delivering three attacks on the Heinkel as it crossed East Lothian. During the last of these, his own aircraft was covered in oil pouring from one of the bomber's engines. He watched as the

German's landing lights were switched on before it crashed in the sea off Barns Ness, south of Dunbar.

A naval trawler picked up three survivors and the pilot, Unteroffizer Wilm, stated that the first volley of anti-aircraft fire from West Pilton had sealed their fate. It was his first mission over the area and he told his interrogators that he 'would not like to come to the Forth again!'

The last of the raiders was moving eastwards past Turnhouse when it was attacked by George Denholm, now in command of 603 Squadron. It jettisoned incendiary bombs near Haddington before disappearing out to sea with one engine smoking.

This last action passed over the south of the city and led to excited Edinburghers phoning the police with groundless reports of crashed aircraft and of parachutists landing near Liberton. Two troops of the 3rd Cavalry Training Regiment were condemned to spending the rest of the night on a fruitless search of the area. The Edinburgh Corporation Gas Department reported that only 65 per cent of its trained ARP staff had turned out for duty on the sirens. Whilst a number had cited 'relatives at home in a hysterical condition' as the reason for not appearing, 25 per cent had simply refused to attend at all.

For the Edinburgh and Glasgow pilots, this was a curiously domestic conflict. Sandy Johnstone's wife, Margaret, was sharing Hillview Cottage at Gullane with Claire Saul, wife of Air Vice-Marshal Richard 'Birdie' Saul, the Air Officer Commanding, 13 Group. Having landed and shaken off an eager intelligence officer, Sandy Johnstone telephoned his wife to ask if she had seen him attack the bomber overhead. 'What did you think of that?' he demanded. There was a pregnant pause. 'What did I think of what?' she replied. Mindful of Birdie Saul's threat to stop their gin ration unless they took to the shelter during an alert, both wives had missed the action.

Further raids took place from 2300 hours on 26 June. At 2339 hours five bombs and 30 incendiaries were dropped at Eagle Rock and Long Green, west of Dalmeny House where 20 panes of glass were shattered. Sandy Johnstone was already airborne and army personnel at Leith Fort watched as he chased the fleeing bomber out to sea. The Heinkel was lost in cloud before it could be brought down. Reports came in that somebody had been seen signalling to the bomber from Eagle Rock.

Two enemy reconnaissance aircraft were detected approaching North Berwick at 1935 hours on Monday, 1 July. Blue Section, 602 Squadron, intercepted one, a JU 88 of 1(F)/121, at 6,000 feet east of Dunbar. At 2005 hours the German dropped his bombs on the foreshore at Belhaven and there followed a chase in and out of cloud during which Johnstone as Blue Leader and his number three, Paul Webb, fired a total of 2,400 rounds. The Junkers eventually crashed in northern France.

Luftwaffe records show that a Junkers 88 of KG 30 failed to return from a mission to the Forth on 7 July. This was one of a pair intercepted at 1813 hours by Hector McLean and Findlay Boyd of 602 Squadron 25 miles east of May Island. At 1935 on 8 July Paul Webb and Sandy Johnstone had an inconclusive engagement with a Heinkel 17 miles east of St Abbs Head. Early on the morning of 9 July a train was bombed near Crail and, that evening, Dunlop Urie despatched another JU 88 into the sea off Fife Ness. Twelve 'Butterfly' anti-personnel bombs fell around Auchtermuchty Police Station just after midnight on 17 July.

Twenty-four raids were mounted against the East Coast on 18 July 1940, mainly against convoys. Bombs were dropped on both Montrose and Crail airfields and, although little damage was done at Crail, two servicemen were killed at Montrose. At 2007 hours, 25 minutes after the raid on Crail, 12 bombs were dropped at Leith. Two fell in the sea, one demolished the west end of No. 6 shed at Victoria Dock and a 250kg bomb landed on the pavement at the junction of Commercial Street and Portland Street. A 50kg bomb fell in Nicoll Place, but failed to explode. Further 50kg bombs fell on 13 George Street, 8 George Street, on a water tower in the LMS Railway Coal Depot and on railway embankments beside Haw-thornvale.

In Commercial Street the bomb fell only yards from tramway car No. 365. Twenty-eight of its windows were shattered and two setts were embedded in its roof. Twenty passengers were uninjured, as were two children playing in the street where sections of manganese steel tramline were thrown up to 60 feet, setts were scattered and windows smashed.

The bomb at 13 George Street pierced the concrete roof of a brick shelter in the back green before exploding. Seventeen-year-old Jane Rutherford was killed and several people injured. At 8 George Street the bomb glanced down the roof before exploding over the

Six people died as a result of the bomb on 8 George Street, Leith.
(HERALD AND EVENING TIMES)

common stair. The building collapsed and six people were killed. The last body, that of 33-year-old David Duff, was not recovered from the wreckage until over 60 hours after the explosion. One man, trapped against a wall by a pile of furniture, was released unharmed by a rescue squad. As Alexander Marshall told a reporter, 'there was a loud explosion and we were lifted off our seats and nearly hit the ceiling'. He and his wife managed to scramble their way out, battering down a neighbour's door to free a mother and her six-year-old son.

Two days later, at 0220 hours on 20 July, a pair of land mines exploded at Stirling injuring 32 people. One of the mines blew the roof off the grandstand at Forthbank football ground, demolished a cottage and so seriously damaged five blocks in a terrace that they were condemned. The other came down just outside the Ordnance Depot at Bandeath. Windows were broken over a large area. A correspondent in the *Stirling Observer* that week suggested that the raid was caused by 'poor people' in Raploch showing lights during the blackout. This drew a sharp response the following week, in which the writer was asked if 'he ever watched the toffs in the terraces!'

Later that morning, parachute mines were dropped in the river near Inchkeith, four of which were exploded by minesweepers in the afternoon. Bombs also fell at Chapel, north of Kirkcaldy.

At 0559 hours on 22 July 1940 a 1000kg bomb was dropped on railway track at the south-west corner of Albert Dock in Leith. A wooden Auxiliary Fire Service (AFS) hut, 45 feet from the explosion, was demolished. Robert Hume (33) of Glover Street, Leith, was killed and eight other firemen injured. A 50kg bomb which exploded near the south-east corner of Edinburgh Dock was followed by two more at Seafield rail junction. A large number of incendiaries were also dropped on the Seafield area, mainly in the cemetery. Among the many premises damaged was Mother Aitken's bar in Salamander Street where the windows were blown out. In requesting the services of a Corporation Repair Party, Bernard's Brewery pointed out that 'the very nature of the business calls for urgency'.

Early the next morning a number of enemy aircraft were operating over the Forth and, at 0023 hours, one dropped 100 incendiaries around Granton Harbour. A number of people were injured including a Mrs Aird who was overcome by fumes as she watched from a window. A seven-day-old infant and his mother were taken to the Western General Hospital suffering from shock. One incendiary bounced out of a front garden into a tenement bedroom where it lay fizzing and sparking on the floor as the occupants made good their escape. AFS personnel and local residents soon had the fires under control. It was thought at the time that the real target was Granton Gasworks which may have been mistaken for oil installations. Bombs were also dropped near Drone Hill radar station where the only casualty was a cow.

Sergeant Andy MacDowall of 602 Squadron was on night patrol at 0035 on Wednesday, 24 July, when he saw a Heinkel held in the beams of searchlights at East Linton. He made a head-on attack and saw tracer enter the enemy aircraft. The intruder immediately jettisoned two parachute mines, one of which exploded at the side of the road past Traprain Law Quarry where it burst a water main and brought down telephone cables. The other blew a large crater in a nearby potato field.

The sight of parachutes dropping from the night sky brought a somewhat agitated signalman at East Linton on the telephone to Waverley Station. He reported that two parachutists had landed nearby and were throwing stones at his window! Even the crew of an anti-aircraft battery at Whitekirk were convinced that enemy parachutists were wandering East Lothian.

The 12,000-ton Salvesen tanker *Salvestria* strayed out of the swept channel on 27 July, triggered a magnetic mine north-east of Inchkeith and sank with the loss of ten of her 57 crew. She had come in with one of the first transatlantic convoys, HX 55A.

On Friday, 4 August, at 0130 hours, an aircraft which had roamed unchallenged over Bathgate, Lanark, Moffat, Peebles and the Lammermuirs dropped five bombs around Abercorn Park, Portobello, all of which failed to explode. Two had fallen in the park itself, one buried itself in the front garden of 84 Argyle Crescent, one came down at 9 Abercorn Terrace and one at the junction of Christian Place and Argyle Place. Mary Dick and her eight children were among 150 evacuated to St Philip's Church Hall. With her she had 2lb of sausages, bread and other supplies so that, as she told a reporter, 'we won't go hungry!'

August and September 1940 saw the Battle of Britain reach its climax. Raids against south-east Scotland were considerably reduced in intensity as Luftwaffe units were moved to France to play their part. Much of the German effort was, in any case, expended against the so-called 'Q' sites. These were decoy sites around the city, at Drem, Ratho, Turnhouse, Earlsferry and Falkland, which were illuminated to present attractive targets.

Twelve aircraft were detected minelaying over the river on the night of 5 September. At 2320 hours, a bright flash and a violent explosion rattled windows over a wide area. From debris which fell to earth it was clear that a minelaying aircraft had blown up on its own cargo. The previous day, however, the tug *Saucy* had blown up on a mine near Inchkeith.

Army units in the Edinburgh area went on full anti-invasion alert at 2240 hours on 7 September. The following day, two ships, the *Stork* and the *Stad Vlaardingen*, were damaged when a pair of

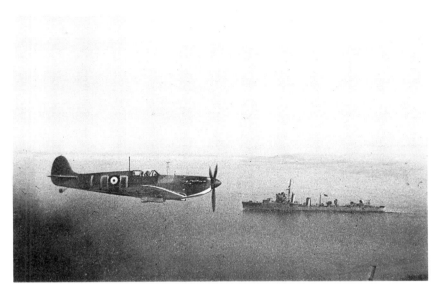

A Spitfire of 602 Squadron on Forth Area Patrol in 1940. Below is one of the old V&W class destroyers dating from the First World War which were used to escort the east coast convoys. Judging from her four-inch high-angle anti-aircraft armament, this particular ship is almost certainly HMS Valorous. Valorous escorted the Polish submarine Orzel into Rosyth following her epic escape from internment at Tallinn in Estonia. Valorous was also, along with the sloop Hastings, a target during the first air attack on ships in the Forth on 27 September 1939. She survived the war and was present at the liberation of Norwegian ports in 1945.
Valorous's sister ship, HMS Viceroy, depth charged and destroyed the U 1274 south east of Berwick on Tweed on 16 April 1945. Viceroy was broken up at Granton in 1947.

(602 SQUADRON ARCHIVES)

seaplanes attacked the convoy anchorage at Methil. The damaged ships were beached but not before one of them had run amok in the anchorage colliding with another ship, the *Algorab*.

Dunbar Railway Station and a searchlight post at Haddington were strafed at 2130 hours on the 9 September. On the 14th five trawlers were attacked off North Berwick and, at 2217 hours on the 15th, a Heinkel 115 seaplane was brought down just over seven miles off Eyemouth by naval anti-aircraft fire. A convoy was attacked off Dunbar the following day and the steamer *Halland* sunk. The *Halland*, an ex-Dutch vessel, was on her way to Dundee with a cargo of cement, 17 of her crew were killed and the survivors brought in to Methil by the trawler *Sparta*. The trawler *Sunbeam III* was also damaged by a mine off Inchkeith.

One bomb fell at the west end of Kinnear Road in the Stewarts-Melville sports ground at 1958 hours on Friday, 27 September. Another exploded 14 minutes later in Holyrood Park, between the Palace and Abbeyhill. Enterprising residents of Abbeyhill charged visitors 1d to gaze on the crater which had revealed ancient foundations. The proceeds went to the Spitfire Fund.

In the early hours of Sunday, 29 September, a raid was tracked up the west coast from Keswick to Carlisle and on towards Edinburgh. After circling over the city for some time, parachute flares were dropped, one of which landed at 57 Sighthill Drive. At 0515 hours, it dropped one 500kg bomb on the Caledonian Distillery at the corner of Duff Street and Springwell Place. Under fire from anti-aircraft batteries at Liberton and West Pilton, it also dropped incendiaries in Belford Road, on a tannery in the Dean Village from where a horse had to be rescued, and in Dean Cemetery.

The distillery housed over a million gallons of whisky and a huge fire started within seconds, flames and smoke leaping hundreds of feet in the air. Hundreds were made homeless when the fire spread to tenements in Duff Street, Springwell Place and Downfield Place. At 0800 hours ARP Warden Charles Boog Watson recorded that a considerable fire was still raging. Earlier he had watched in awe as the flames had silhouetted Roseburn Church against the night sky. Later, the Dutch steamer *Arizona* struck a mine and sank one mile south of Kincraig Point. Five of her crew were killed.

That night a single aircraft dropped one bomb from around 20,000 feet which scored a direct hit on a block of flats at 27 Crewe Place. Mrs McArthur was blown out of her house by the force of the blast. Rescue workers toiled for two hours to extricate her children, Ronald (8) and Moira (6), only to find Ronald already dead and Moira, who had been partially shielded by her brother's body, grievously injured. She died in the ambulance on the way to the Western General Hospital.

Also fatally injured was Charles Wilson of 25 Crewe Place. Seven people were seriously injured and another 23 lightly so. One man had a particularly lucky escape when, on hearing the aircraft, he got up to go outside. After the explosion he turned round to find

*Survivors pick through the wreckage of miners' cottages in Main Street, Kelty,
following the raid on 4 November 1940.*
(HERALD AND EVENING TIMES)

that the room he had just left had vanished leaving the door
swinging drunkenly on its hinges.

This aircraft also dropped a bomb near a searchlight post at
Portobello Mains. Two Hurricanes of 141 Squadron were scrambled to intercept the raider but no contact was made.

War came to the Meadows on Monday, 7 October 1940, when,
at 1945 hours, a stick of five 50kg bombs was dropped. The first
of these failed to explode after glancing off the gable ends of both
29 Roseneath Terrace and 20 Meadow Place. It buried itself four
feet under the slabs covering Meadow Place. The four other bombs
did explode. Two fell at 16 Roseneath Place, one of them landing
in the street outside, one at 13 Marchmont Crescent and the other

*Two land mines exploded in Leith at 2130 hours on 7 April 1941, killing three
and injuring over 130. One of the mines demolished the infant's annexe of
David Kilpatrick's School and caused considerable damage to the adjacent Concert Hall as seen here.*

*The other mine exploded on the railway embankment next to Largo Place and
repairs to the retaining wall are still clearly visible over 50 years later. Shrapnel
damage and repairs to the front of 16 Roseneath Place resulting from the raid
on 7 October 1940 can still be seen, as can repairs to gable ends in nearby
Meadow Place, necessary after an unexploded bomb had bounced off them
that same night.*

(HERALD AND EVENING TIMES)

behind 21 Marchmont Road. Eleven people were slightly injured,
mostly by flying glass, and a number of children found themselves
taking an extra bath after soot was dislodged from chimneys and
fell on their beds.

According to a Ministry of Home Security report, the public
'displayed a great reluctance to move from the scene of the incident,
and the work of the Civil Defence services was rather hampered'.
The air- raid alert sounded six minutes after the bombs dropped.

A German communiqu issued the next day stated that 'large fires were observed' in Edinburgh following the previous night's raid. A German propaganda film doing the rounds in the occupied countries, which claimed to show air-raid damage in Edinburgh, was actually taken in Rotterdam.

There was also considerable enemy activity over the river that night as mines were dropped at Methil. What one observer described as 'a great flash in the sky', along with the sound of an explosion, was thought to have been caused by the mid-air explosion of a parachute mine. Two days later the motor boat *Girl Mary* was mined off Incholm and two of her crew killed.

Crail came under attack again at 1055 on 18 October when five high explosive bombs and two oil bombs were dropped by a Junkers 88. One house was badly damaged and two people injured, one seriously. The bomber also exchanged machine-gun fire with a searchlight post in fields west of the town. Crail was again the target on the 24th at 0445 when two mines exploded at Redwells Wood. Bombs also fell at Leslie, Aberdour and Tulliallan. A mine exploded in the sea at East Bay, North Berwick, shattering many windows in the town. Other raiders scattered bombs and mines at Dennyloanhead, Stirling and Grangemouth. At 0411 hours Totley Wells battery near Winchburgh opened fire on a bomber illuminated by searchlights.

A further attack on Crail took place at 1855 hours on 25 October when eight bombs were dropped by a low flying Heinkel 111. The first was a direct hit on a shepherd's cottage at Backfields Farm, Kilrenny which killed both 12-year-old Douglas Scott and his mother. Earlier, on 9 July 1940, the Scotts' cottage had suffered damage in one of the first raids on the Forth. Another bomb caused

Following page:
On 8 March 1941 this party of largely boy seamen from the battle cruiser HMS Hood *visited Broomhall, the Earl of Elgin's home near Limekilns in Fife. Just over two months later 1418 lives were lost when* Hood *simply disintegrated in one colossal explosion after a shell from the German battleship* Bismarck *exploded in a magazine under X turret at 0637 hours on 24 May 1941. Some days laater HMS* Prince of Wales, *which had been working with* Hood *at the time of the explosion, arrived at Rosyth for repair. She still had substantial pieces of the* Hood *embedded in her decks.*
Bismarck *was finally sent to the bottom at 1101 hours on 27 May by torpedoes from the cruiser HMS* Dorsetshire.
(BY KIND PERMISSION OF THE EARL OF ELGIN)

Wm Burmingham C.P.O G.M. H.M.S. HOOD
8th March 1941

G. Myers Boy 1/c

E. J. Holmes. Boy 1/c

P. J. Palmer. Boy 1/c

H. Byrne Boy 1/c

Wm Kim Boy 1/c

M. R. Douglass. Boy 1/c

L. Finch Boy 1/c

G. V. Collis Boy 1/c

Anthony V Read Boy 1/c
H.M.S "Hood"

D. Kennerry

P. C. Long Boy 1/c

J. Donald Boy 1/c
H.M.S. Hood

cref.

a. Bullard.
Boy 1/c
H.M.S. HOOD

J. J. Walsh

S. Rootham

H. Mills

J. W. Lambert

H.M.S.
HOOD.

VENTIS SECUNDIS

considerable damage to houses in Rodger Street and one failed to explode after falling in a garden in West Forth Street. A mine exploded off Anstruther and a bomb at Kinghorn.

Early the next morning, at 0344 hours, anti-aircraft guns were in action against a bomber caught in searchlights over Rosyth. South Queensferry ARP post had watched as it dropped a flare and a bomb at Donibristle. Later, at 0525 hours, two bombs exploded near Pencaitland. These were followed by five, all UXBs (unexploded bombs), at Windymains, near Humbie, and East Linton. At East Linton, one went through the concrete pavement of the bridge over the River Tyne and fell 40 feet to the river bed below. Another buried itself in a nearby lawn. The village and station were strafed, bullets damaging the roofs of houses in the Main Street. Nobody was injured though nine children, described in the uncompromising terms of the time as 'mentally defective', who had been evacuated to a house overlooking the by-pass bridge, were to be found safer billets.

In Edinburgh that night, 26 October 1940, a stray anti-aircraft shell exploded inside a flat at 2 West Norton Place. Mr and Mrs Greig, the occupants, were sheltering along with their two children in a lower flat. Next door, Mrs Cochrane threw an overcoat over herself and her two children for protection from blast and shrapnel. Bombs and mines also fell near Eskbank and Balerno, and a searchlight post at Methil was machine-gunned.

On the 27th, at 2201 hours, a raider was caught in searchlights off Methil and immediately came under anti-aircraft fire from Inchkeith. It returned fire down the beams of searchlights before turning tail. It had clearly suffered damage as, after emitting a red glow, it blew up in full view of spectators on Methil promenade. That same night the drifter *Persevere* blew up on a mine near the Dunnet Ledge Buoy in the river.

The first three days of November brought scattered raids during which bombs landed, particularly in Fife and around Penicuik and Currie. The patrol drifter *Goodwill* was mined and sunk off Inchkeith at 1155 hours on the 2nd. At 2000 hours on the 4th pedestrians in Corstorphine ran for cover as shrapnel rained down on the west end. Despite the heavy barrage, a raider dropped six bombs across Corstorphine and machine-gunned the streets.

The bombs, all 250kg, fell on Pinkhill House, in the zoo, in a quarry at the north end of Kaimes Road and in the grounds of

Clermiston House. In the zoo one bomb fell close to an aviary killing six budgerigars. Glass was also broken in the reptile house and the ape house suffered damage. None of the nine chimps or two orang-utans were injured though, as Zoo Director T. H. Gillespie wrote, 'If their bodies did not suffer, I am afraid their tempers did, for they kept up a loud chorus of indignation for a considerable period.' Another bomb fell close to an aviary housing ravens and golden eagles but did only superficial damage.

Bombs also fell close to the laundry and boilerhouse at the Royal Scottish National Hospital in Larbert, and at Carronshore near Falkirk. Here, one which buried itself at Yonderhaugh Farm only exploded some hours later.

Other minor raids took place that night at Dunbar, Falkland, Newburgh and Kelty. Four bombs exploded at Kingseat in Fife at 2130 hours At 78 Main Street a direct hit on the house killed Thomas Pollock. He had left the shelter to see to the kitchen fire. In the back garden, the shelter he had just left was thrown 80 feet off its foundations and buried under earth blown up by another bomb which exploded alongside it. The occupants had to be dragged out through small holes dug by rescue workers. Two blocks of single-storey cottages were destroyed and eight families made homeless. One woman had a lucky escape when a large piece of debris crashed through the roof of her cottage, landing on her bed. She complained of a headache the following day.

November 1940 was an eventful month for the fishing drifter *Violet*. In the afternoon of the 6th she was working off Anstruther when a mine exploded in her nets. On the night of the 13th a large number of enemy aircraft were detected minelaying over the river and, two days later, the *Violet* towed a parachute mine into shallow water off Fidra. That same afternoon the drifter *Jean Edmunds* exploded an acoustic mine near Inchkeith and was swamped. She was towed in and beached at Granton. On the 22nd the steam lighter *Glen* blew up and disappeared while carrying ammunition between Grangemouth and Crombie and, the following day, the motor patrol boat *Good Design* was mined near Inchkeith and four of its crew of six killed.

At 1800 hours on the 26th two bombs were dropped at Binn Grange Farm, quarter of a mile from the British Aluminium Works at Burntisland. Home Guardsmen returned fire using machine-guns mounted on the factory roof. A German communiqu later claimed hits on an armaments factory. Prestonkirk Poorhouse at East Linton was damaged the following night when three bombs fell nearby, one coming down in the garden and breaking windows.

The sirens sounded at 0606 hours on Friday 29 November just as Raid 233 dropped several bombs on the foreshore off Dalmeny House. This raider dropped 150 incendiaries near Penicuik before returning to the south west over the Mull of Galloway.

After four months in the front line at Hornchurch airfield, east of London, 603 Squadron returned to home territory in December 1940. They had been severely mauled during the Battle of Britain, losing 12 pilots and 16 aircraft between 25 August and 5 September. At 1255 hours on Christmas Day, Brian Carbury led Blue Section up on patrol. Shortly afterwards they intercepted a JU 88 off St Abbs Head. Carbury attacked twice and the bomber disappeared into cloud with its undercarriage down and its starboard engine stopped.

The commodore ship of convoy EN74, the SS *Athel Sultan*, took a direct hit when she was attacked by a JU 88 off Anstruther at 1055 hours on 19 February 1941. Lieutenant Brown in the escort trawler *Lady Rosemary* returned fire with a Hotchkiss machine-gun. *Athel Sultan* was forced to return to Methil and then Leith for repairs.

On Monday, 3 March, her sister ship, the *Athel Templar*, arrived at Leith. She had been badly damaged in an air attack off the north-east coast. Eighteen wounded crewmen had been transferred to a trawler and landed at Aberdeen. Still on board were 17 survivors and five bodies, only one of which could be identified. So gruesome was the sight which greeted shipyard workers that a firm of undertakers was immediately called in to remove the remains.

At 2030 hours that night the sirens sounded the alert over Haddington but, after three months of relative quiet it had become almost impossible to motivate the public to take cover. At 2100 hours wardens were complaining that Amisfield Park was lit up 'like a fairyland'. A large number of hurricane lamps were being used in troop movements. Seven minutes later a line of flares was dropped along the River Tyne. A number of incendiaries then fell along the High Street followed by five high explosive bombs also in the High Street and in Hardgate. The raiders carried on to the east dropping incendiaries near East Linton.

35 Loaning Road, Craigentinny, following the raid on 6 August 1942. Rescue Party personnel, some of whom are seen here, had made desperate efforts to rescue 13-year-old Betty Veitch, who was buried under the wreckage, alive. They were not successful.
(HERALD AND EVENING TIMES)

Water and gas mains were ruptured by a bomb which had produced a crater twelve feet wide by four feet deep in the High Street. The cinema, which was full at the time, suffered a near miss. Fierce fires started almost immediately and it became apparent that the local fire service would require assistance. The first two requests for reinforcements were ignored as they had not been made through the proper channels, this despite the fire threatening a building used to store ammunition and Molotov cocktails and a petrol station.

The collapse of telephone communications was a very real possibility and the women running the exchange stayed at their posts despite a bomb having exploded only yards away. So intense was the heat from the fires that curtains inside the exchange caught fire and had to be put out using a stirrup pump.

Butcher Frank Anderson, who lived over his shop in the High Street, looked out and saw an incendiary bomb blazing in the back yard. He hurried downstairs and extinguished it with sand. Just then he heard a crash and found that a bomb had glanced off the roof of the newspaper office next door and gone clean through the side wall of his house before coming to rest, without exploding, on his doormat. Mrs Anderson and the children stepped over the bomb on their way out and, assisted by Inspector Birrell of the local police, Mr Anderson carried the bomb downstairs and out into the yard. It was later made safe by bomb disposal personnel.

Two people were killed: John Moggie of Amisfield Stables and Sergeant J. Mathieson of the 52nd Division, both of whom were hit by debris. Among those seriously injured were George Scott of Victoria Terrace and Alison Young of 25 Sprotlands Crescent, most of the injuries being due to people still being on the streets despite the sirens.

As the attacks were mounted against the Clyde Valley during March 1941 little effort was made against targets around the Forth. Two workmen were injured by splinters at Crail airfield at 1230 hours on the 8th during a hit-and-run raid in which three hangars were also damaged. Mines and high explosive bombs were dropped at Slamannan, Maddiston, High Bonnybridge near Falkirk and near Grangemouth on the 13th. A Drem-based Blenheim of 600 (County of London) Squadron shot down a HE 111 of KG 100 south of Glasgow at 2151 on 13 March. KG 100 was the Luftwaffe's lite pathfinder unit. Pilot Officer Denby's victim was, however, many miles off course. Seventy incendiaries were dropped around Abbey-hill in Edinburgh on the 14th, the Norwegian ship *Einar Jarl* was sunk off May Island on the 17th and the submarine *Seawolf* was unsuccessfully bombed off Dunbar on the 30th.

At 1404 hours on 2 April the Auxiliary Patrol trawler *Cramond Island* was bombed and sunk off St Abbs Head. Wounded survivors were picked up by Eyemouth lifeboat. The *Fortuna*, another trawler which was sent to assist, simply disappeared. Two bodies were later washed ashore near Eyemouth. The JU 88 responsible was subsequently attacked and damaged off Alnmouth by Flight Lieutenant Young of 317 Squadron.

The next major attack took place on Monday, 7 April 1941. Widespread but poorly directed raids resulted in bombs and mines being scattered over farmland from Fife to the Borders. In Fife these were dropped at or near Dunfermline, Inverkeithing, Burntisland, Markinch, Leslie and Cowdenbeath. In the Lothians, Ratho, Niddrie Oil Works in Kirkliston, Dalmeny, Linlithgow, Mid Calder and the N.B. Foundry at Bathgate were targets.

Extensive damage was caused by the first of two land mines dropped at 2130 hours that night in Leith. It scored a direct hit on the infants' annexe of David Kilpatrick's School where three of the six shelters in the playground collapsed. The second mine fell on the railway embankment opposite 5 Largo Place where a crater 27 feet wide and five feet deep was made and two tenements seriously damaged. Here 19-year-old Kenneth Anderson was killed. His brother and two sisters were injured along with his mother, Cecilia Anderson.

Janet Young (84) of 21 North Junction Street died of shock. The other fatal casualty that night was 17-year-old Ernest Smith, an air-raid messenger. The sirens sounded four minutes after the mines exploded.

Thirty-seven people were seriously injured and a further 95 required first aid, many of these injuries being caused by flying glass. Shop windows were blown out and a number of fires started both by incendiaries and coals blown out of grates. The piano stood on stage in the concert hall, surrounded by debris, and all the glass in the library was smashed. Twelve houses were demolished, 40 were seriously damaged and a further 500 required minor repairs. Six hundred people were made homeless. Incendiaries dropped at Corstorphine and at Braehead House, Cramond, were quickly dealt with.

The HQ and billets of the 8th (HD) KOSB at Greenlaw were hit at 0005 hours on 8 April. Four were killed and six wounded. One bomb fell on the Touch Waterworks at Stirling, four at Canada Cottages in Camelon, three at Seafield Farm, Falkirk, and one at Coxhill Farm, Maddiston. At 0630 hours on the 9th, Belgian Battle of Britain veteran, Pilot Officer Le Roy du Vivier, was one of two 43 Squadron pilots in action with a JU 88 two miles off North Berwick.

Over the next month minor raids took place during which North Berwick gasworks and a searchlight post near Dirleton were unsuccessfully attacked.

The Luftwaffe mounted a second mass attack against Clydeside on Tuesday 6 and Wednesday 7 May 1941, during which Greenock was particularly badly hit. At 0036 hours on the 6th, four bombs were dropped on Niddrie Road and Milton Crescent. The aircraft responsible was crossing the city towards Glasgow when it was caught by searchlights and damaged by anti-aircraft fire.

Firewatchers Joseph Watson, Leonard Wilde and William Dineley, all from Milton Crescent, were killed after taking cover between the east gable wall of 35 Milton Crescent and an adjacent concrete shelter, when a bomb exploded nearby. Barbara Thomson, an 86-year-old invalid of 30 Niddrie Road, was killed when a large lump of clay, thrown up by a 1,000kg bomb which exploded in the field behind her house, came through the roof and landed on her bed. One hundred incendiaries dropped around Jewel Cottages on Niddrie Road were soon extinguished.

Earlier, at 0001 hours, Squadron-Leader Morgan of 43 Squadron shot down a JU 88 off Anstruther. He was back on patrol at 0150 hours when he brought down another bomber. Morgan scored his third victory 24 hours later when he shot down another JU 88 off St Abbs Head. At 2235 hours on the 10th a lone Messerschmidt 110 blasted low over Selkirk, heading west. At 2306 hours it crashed in a field near Eaglesham, south of Glasgow. The pilot was Rudolph Hess. 43 Squadron were in action again at 1415 hours on 28 May, Red Section shooting down a JU 88 south of Hawick. Two of the crew survived and were taken to Jedburgh Police Station.

Seven were killed at Berwick on Tweed on the night of 1 June 1941 and on the 3rd, the *Royal Fusilier* was bombed near the Bass Rock while on her way from London to Leith with a cargo of rice and paper. She sank shortly afterwards while under tow. On the 8th, Squadron Leader Morgan shot down another JU 88 15 miles off St Abbs Head.

HMS *Liddesdale* and HMS *Versatile* engaged an HE 111 at 0205 hours on 25 June after it dropped bombs near the convoy they were escorting past Fife Ness. Pom-pom fire from *Liddesdale* was clearly seen to hit the bomber and it crashed. *Versatile* picked up the German crew from their dinghy and gave them minor first-aid. At first they were described as 'surly' though they started to chatter in

English when they were given breakfast and confirmed that they had been hit just after dropping their bombs. On arrival at Rosyth they were blindfolded prior to being handed over to a military escort. As *Versatile*'s Captain put it, 'The blindfolds shook them as they thought that they were a prelude to a firing squad!'

A Junkers 88 (A6+BH) of 1(F)/120 was shot down off May Island by the Hurricanes of Squadron-Leader Morgan and Pilot Officer Bourne of 43 Squadron at 1625 hours on 24 July 1941, and a raid at Spittal in August killed six and injured eight.

A lone JU 88 attacked a party of railwaymen at Innerwick Station at 1430 hours on 17 August 1941. It dropped two 250kg bombs, both of which failed to explode. One hit the parapet wall of the bridge. The other passed through the arch of the bridge, bounced 400 yards down the line and into a potato field. One man was killed and three injured by machine-gun fire from the bomber which went on to strafe Dunbar. Earlier, 43 Squadron had scored a further success by downing another JU 88 off St Abbs Head.

The steam trawler *Craddock* was attacked 14 miles north-east of St Abbs Head at 1830 on the 8th. Bombed and strafed by one of four JU 88s operating in the area, she sank and the crew were picked up by another trawler. The *Flying Scotsman* was strafed near Berwick on Tweed two weeks later.

Two JU 88s were brought down off St Abbs Head by Wing-Commander Meagher at 1230 hours on 19 December. Meagher was on a non-operational sortie from Turnhouse and, having shot one of the bombers down, watched as it collided with its companion.

Another Junkers appeared off the coast near Berwick on 4 January 1942. It was heard by the 'Y', or radio interception service, to be passing back information on Convoy 'Numeral' before dropping two bombs at Tweedmouth which demolished several houses, damaged some army huts and left four dead. Three people were injured by three bombs dropped at Eyemouth harbour at 1910 hours on 31 January.

Three enemy aircraft were detected approaching from the south-east at 2230 on 6 August 1942. Turning inland over Dunbar, one went north and dropped four bombs at St Andrews. At 2320 hours, 12 minutes after the sirens had sounded, another bomber passed at about 1,000 feet along the north side of Loaning Road in Craigentinny. Four 500kg bombs were dropped. The first ripped off the gable end of a tenement at 35 Loaning Road, another caused considerable blast damage to tenements at 29 Loaning Road and 1 Loaning Crescent, and two wrecked the east wing of Craigentinny House.

The ground-floor flat at 35 Loaning Road was devastated by the explosion. Elizabeth Veitch and her two-year-old daughter were taken to the Eastern General Hospital with serious injuries. Betty Veitch (13) was buried under rubble and, despite the frantic efforts of rescue workers, she was dead when found two hours later.

Robert Wright, the caretaker at Craigentinny House, was also found dead in the wreckage of his quarters. The last bomb demolished two unoccupied concrete shelters belonging to Nimmo's Hosiery factory. Ten minutes later four bombs exploded in the sea off Port Seton. The all clear sounded at 2345 hours. Three hundred and forty-five people whose homes had been damaged or destroyed were initially looked after at St Christopher's Church Hall and St Ninian's Rest Centre.

The Luftwaffe's last two visits to the Forth took place early on Thursday 25 March 1943 and 5 May 1944. During the former, the first alert since 25 August 1942, a large number of phosphorus incendiaries fell on farmland near Balerno. Other mixed bombs were dropped near Drem airfield, near Kelty in Fife, at Dalmeny Home Farm and in the Borders. Four JU 88s made the mistake of passing over West Pilton battery which was by then manned by the Home Guard. From Garscube Terrace, Charles Boog Watson could see 'a tremendous blaze of gunfire in the north' which was accompanied by a deafening noise. Three bombers were shot down. One crashed at Hare Hill near Balerno, and two crashed in the river after exploding in mid-air. More bombers crashed at Earlston in Berwickshire and in Kirkcudbrightshire.

The high-speed, low-level strafing attack by a lone JU 188 on Edinburgh's streets in May 1944 came as a considerable surprise. It was, however, to be the Kriegsmarine which would launch the last three attacks against the River Forth.

The type VIIC U-boat *U 714,* sank the Swedish ship *Magme* in a convoy off Eyemouth on 14 March 1945 before she was herself depth-charged and sunk six-and-a-half miles off St Abbs Head by HMS *Wyvern* and the South African Navy frigate *Natal.* Four days earlier *U 714* had sunk the Norwegian minesweeper *Nordhav II* off the mouth of the Tay. The 1,406-ton steamship *Gasray* of the Gas, Light and Coke Company was on passage from Grangemouth to

Blyth when she was torpedoed two miles off St Abbs Head on 5 April 1945.

At 2300 hours on 7 May 1945, one hour before the formal German surrender took effect, *U 2336*, a Type XXIII boat under the command of Kapitanleutnant Emil Klusemeyer, intercepted a convoy one mile east of May Island. He sank two ships, the *Avondale Park* and the Norwegian *Sneland I* before successfully returning to Germany to surrender. Nine men were pointlessly killed. Thus it was the Firth of Forth, and in particular May Island, which saw both the very first and the very last enemy action against mainland Britain during the Second World War.

Chapter Five

'Who was the Bloody Fool who Thought up Such a Silly Code Word?'

The Banffshire coastline was shrouded in darkness when the Heinkel 115 seaplane ploughed to a halt a short distance offshore. Two men and a woman climbed down into a rubber dinghy which had been hurriedly inflated and dropped into the sea. Suitcases were passed down as the dinghy bounced around on an uncomfortably choppy sea. Three bicycles followed but were quickly thrown overboard as their extra weight threatened to swamp the already overloaded boat. Having paddled for a short distance, they turned and watched as their last link with home took off and set course back to Norway.

Cold and wet, their dinghy half full of water, the three struggled ashore at at the mouth of Gollachy Burn, a short distance from the village of Portgordon. The younger of the two men then pushed the dinghy out onto an ebbing tide.

The loss of the bicycles necessitated a change of plans and, as they ate a hasty breakfast on the beach, they consulted their maps by the light of a shaded torch. Picking out the two nearest railway stations, Portgordon to the west and Buckpool to the east, they split up and hurried away into the dawn. Apart from the waves breaking on the shore, the only sound was that of a dog barking at the farmhouse behind the beach.

The events surrounding this early morning landing form a sad tale of naive incompetence. Almost a year later, two of the three would walk to the gallows.

Operation Hummer Nord I was one of a series mounted by the Abwehr, or German Secret Service, to coincide with the planned invasion of Great Britain in September 1940. Four agents were to be landed in north-east Scotland from where they would make their way to eastern England and report on the strength of RAF units stationed there. Though, in theory, this information could be of considerable benefit to an invading force, the sophistication of Abwehr planning can best be judged from the fact that the agents were to use the bicycles to cover the 600 miles to London.

Hastily trained at an Abwehr spy school in Hamburg, the four were due to leave for Norway, their jumping-off point, on 2 September 1940. The previous evening was spent celebrating the completion of their training in a Hamburg restaurant. The party appears to have been a success and it was a distinctly merry group of putative spies which left the restaurant by car. The driver and leader of the party, Captain Hans Dierks, overturned the car in Seirichstrasse and was killed. The rest suffered cuts and bruises.

Though still recovering from their injuries, the remaining three agents were in Stavanger by 26 September when a first attempt to land them in Scotland failed due to bad weather. The successful flight took place early on the morning of Monday, 30 September.

After the whispered farewell on the beach, two of the agents made off to the west. One carried papers describing himself as Francois de Deeker, a refugee born in Brussels in March 1906 and living at 15 Sussex Gardens, London. The other, a young woman, purported to be Vera Erikson, a Dane of 18 Sussex Place, London W2. There would have been few people about to see them make their way slowly towards Portgordon. At around 0730 hours, they arrived at the small railway station.

Stationmaster John Donald was immediately struck by the fact that the young couple seemed completely unaware of their where-abouts. Station name boards had been removed in the belief that this would confuse an invading German army. When she approached the ticket desk Vera Erikson's first question was to ask the name of the station. Examining a timetable on the wall, de Deeker pointed to Forres and Vera, who did most of the talking, asked for two single tickets.

Later, while being interrogated by MI5, de Deeker admitted that he had chosen Forres as it appeared to be a junction where they would have to change and where tickets to London would appear a less conspicuous purchase. De Deeker pulled out his wallet to pay for the tickets and John Donald noticed that it was crammed with notes. Strangers are always conspicuous in a small community such as Portgordon, particularly early in the morning. He had also by this time observed that both his customers were very wet, particularly below the knees. Having sold them their tickets, the station-master instructed his porter, John Geddes, to keep the couple talking while he telephoned the local policeman, Constable Robert Grieve.

Grieve arrived at the station minutes later and asked the couple for their papers. Right away, he spotted that the identity cards had been completed using continental-style handwriting. In addition, despite the claims of his suspects that they were refugees, neither of their identity cards carried the required immigration stamps.

Grieve took the couple the short distance to Portgordon Police Station from where he telephoned his superior, Inspector John Simpson, at Buckie. Arriving at Portgordon, Simpson searched de Deeker and found a box containing 19 rounds of small arms ammunition in his pocket. He, too, noticed the continental handwriting on their identity cards and could not have failed to notice that, numbered CNFQ/141/1 and CNFX/141/2, they were close to being consecutive.

By now certain that he had two enemy agents on his hands, Simpson took them to Buckie Police Station and began a thorough search of their belongings. Vera meanwhile had told him that de Deeker was unable to speak English and that they had come from Bergen in a boat called the *Norstar* captained by a man called Andersen. Unwisely, she told him that they had spent the previous night in a hotel in Banff and had taken a taxi to within a mile of the station, a story all too easy to check. Her protestations of innocence were in any case pointless as their belongings were found to contain, amongst other things, a torch stamped 'Made in Bohemia', a list of RAF bases in eastern England, £327 in Bank of England notes and some German sausage.

Breaking open the suitcase carried by de Deeker, Simpson found it to contain a small calibre Mauser automatic pistol loaded with six rounds, various coding devices and a wireless set complete with morse key.

Simpson reported his find to Police Headquarters at Banff who sent Superintendent George Strath to take charge of the prisoners.

Carrying a Swiss passport describing himself as Werner Heinrich Walti, a chauffeur born at Horgen near Zurich in December 1915,

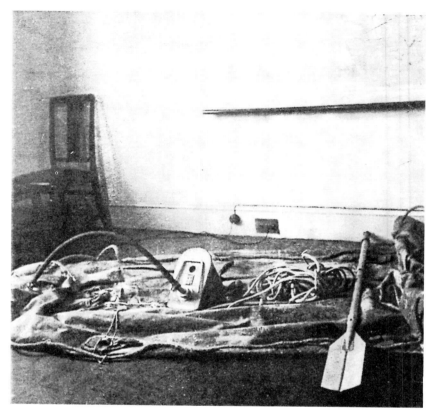

After its recovery from the sea by Buckie coastguards, the dinghy used by the Portgordon spies was taken to MI5 headquarters in London and photographed as part of the evidence to be used at their trial.
(TRUSTEES OF THE NATIONAL MUSEUMS OF SCOTLAND, 1992)

the third agent walked the short distance to Buckpool station where he arrived at 0650 hours. On asking the time of the next train to Aberdeen he was told that one had just left but that one would leave Buckie, a short distance away, at 0958 hours.

Having been given directions, he boarded a bus on which the conductress was unable to change the 10/-(50p) note he offered for the 2d(1p) fare. Arriving at Buckie at around 0745 hours, he bought a ticket for Edinburgh. Seeing him scanning the timetable, Porter Paterson asked him rather quaintly, 'Have you lost a train, sir?'

Walti did not reply but simply showed him the ticket to Edinburgh. With two hours to kill he went for a walk and was seen to board the late-running Aberdeen train at 1004 hours carrying two pieces of luggage, one a large brown suitcase. Little did he know that, at that very moment, his erstwhile companions were but a short distance away in Buckie Police Station, under interrogation.

At around the same time as Walti arrived in Aberdeen, coastguards at Buckie retrieved the waterlogged rubber dinghy which had been seen floating about a quarter of a mile offshore.

Their suspicions about the couple in their custody clearly having good foundation, Police Headquarters at Banff contacted MI5's Regional Security Liaison Officer, Peter Perfect, in Edinburgh. Perfect wasted little time in setting out to drive north. In the days before the Forth and Tay were bridged, this would have taken almost five hours.

By the time he arrived at Buckie, whilst de Deeker had remained uncommunicative, Vera was being more talkative. She had told Inspector Simpson that she was Vera de Cottani Chalbur, a widow of Siberian origin and that a certain Captain King in London would prove her bona fides.

Captain King was one of the many aliases used by none other than Max Knight, the head of MI5's B5b counter-subversion division. Whether Perfect was aware of the significance of this is not clear, however it transpired that before the war, Vera had acted as a low-grade informant for Knight, passing on pieces of society gossip gleaned in the Mayfair hairdressing salon where she worked.

Meanwhile Vera had also informed Perfect that the man arrested with her was really Karl Drugge, an Abwehr agent whom she was to guide to London. She also gave the first confirmation of a third agent when she told Perfect of the existence of a man she knew only as Werner Walti who, she said, had set out to find his own way south. A search of the shore at Portgordon turned up a pair of rubber boots of apparently foreign manufacture, along with the remains of a meal. In addition the farmer at Gollachy Burn told police that his dog had been disturbed early that morning. Further confirmation of Walti's existence came that afternoon from Porter Paterson at Buckie Station who remembered the stranger boarding the Aberdeen train that morning. Enquiries at Aberdeen brought confirmation that a man answering Walti's description had boarded the lunchtime express to Edinburgh. Not until 1710 hours, a full

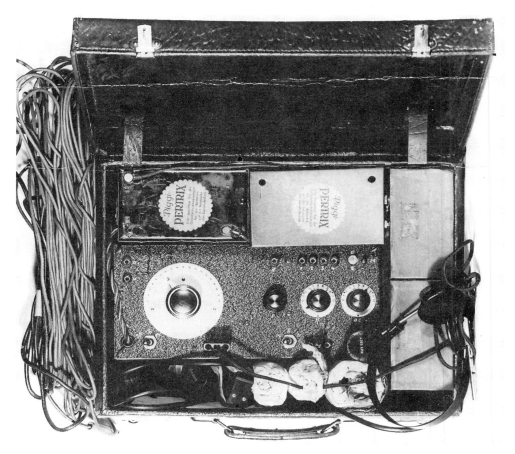

The radio deposited in Waverley Station left luggage office by Werner Walti.
(TRUSTEES OF THE NATIONAL MUSEUMS OF SCOTLAND, 1992)

40 minutes after the train from Aberdeen arrived at Edinburgh, was the officer in charge of the capital's CID, Detective Lieutenant William Merrilees, informed.

In his account of the affair, Merrilees is scathing of the delay in transmitting the information to him. He wasted little time in ordering what he termed an immediate 'comb out' of the city. Enquiries were made at hotels, boarding-houses, even the YMCA. At Waverley Station, sidings were searched and porters were questioned. In the left-luggage office facing platform 19 on the north side of the station, officers came across a salt-stained suitcase. Meanwhile, a destination board attendant had approached a colleague to ask what 'the Splits' were looking for. He told police officers that he had been approached by a young man off the north train who had asked him where he could deposit his luggage. Probably with a tip in mind, he had carried the man's case to the left luggage office but, not being a porter, he had not been questioned. The salt-stained case was forced open to reveal a wireless set of German origin.

Willie Merrilees placed a number of plainclothes officers at strategic points in the station, sometimes accompanied by members of the Women's Voluntary Service as camouflage. He had donned a uniform borrowed from a real porter, Thomas Ferguson.

For three hours the police watched crowds of wartime travellers come and go. In looking for obvious foreigners, their task was not made any easier by the presence of a large number of, for example, Polish soldiers. At around 2100 hours Merrilees became aware of a young man approaching the left luggage office from the Waverley Steps. He asked the destination board attendant to identify the man but, in the blackout, this was not possible. Clearly nervous, the man stood against one of the kiosks opposite the left luggage office for some moments before approaching the counter and handing over his ticket with an imperious 'Now, please'.

While awaiting his luggage, Walti retreated from the counter and stood next to the kiosks. He carried his briefcase in his right hand. His left hand was in his trouser pocket and, approaching his quarry from the shadows of the darkened station, Merrilees was convinced it held a gun.

The fair-haired young man was clearly very scared. He had passed the last five hours in Edinburgh by going first to a barber's for a shave and then to the cinema. Desperately hungry, he had looked in at more than one restaurant but had turned away convinced he would be unable to keep food down. On the train that afternoon, he had listened to his fellow passengers while pretending to read the paperback book he had been given in Stavanger. Watching the crowds in Princes Street that autumn evening, he must have realised that Britain was not a nation on the verge of collapse. A movement caught his eye. Who was that porter waving to?

Walking slowly towards his quarry, Merrilees could see that the young man had fixed him with a wary gaze. He used the old trick of waving supposedly to someone in the distance. When Walti glanced in that direction, 'Wee Willie' leapt forward to grab his left arm, wrenching it out of the pocket to reveal a small calibre Mauser automatic pistol.

For some reason, after disarming him and pushing him into the left luggage office, Merrilees's men failed to take the precaution of handcuffing their captive. In a last despairing attempt to escape, Walti pulled out a flick-knife and brandished it at the detectives searching his belongings. Somewhat less than gently, he was disarmed for a second time and taken to Police Headquarters in, of all things, an ambulance. There he was stripped, searched for possible concealed poison and photographed.

Despite the amount of incriminating evidence found on him, Walti continued to protest his innocence, loudly declaring that he was Swiss and not German. In addition to the wireless, he was discovered to have a primitive cardboard coding disk and a handwritten book containing standard 'Q' code radio-communication abbreviations, which any properly trained operator would have known by heart.

Every bit as incriminating were 14 maps found in his briefcase which covered the eastern half of Britain from Caithness and Sutherland as far south as East Anglia. Some were of German origin, including one covering the 'Ostliches Hochland' of 'Schottland'. Most, however, were standard pre-war Ordnance Survey maps overprinted with both the latest information gathered from aerial reconnaissance, including newly built-up areas, and a Luftwaffe target grid. Among the places of special interest marked are the airfields, described as 'Flugplatz', at Cranfield and Wittering and the airship station at Cardington. The map of the Moray Firth was marked in blue pencil to show areas at which a landing should not be attempted.

He was also carrying a wallet containing the considerable sum for the day of £190, a blank traveller's ration book numbered CA 568427 and, amazingly, a book of graph paper bearing the name of a senior Luftwaffe officer in Norway. His briefcase was also found to contain a box of 25 rounds for the Mauser automatic.

Two particularly bizarre items were found. One was a rather gushy love letter addressed to 'Dear Kurt' and signed 'affectionately, Marion'. The sender's address is given merely as Palo Alto, California. The other was a paperback book entitled *The Substitute*

The forged Swiss passport carried by Robert Petter alias Werner Walti.
(TRUSTEES OF THE NATIONAL MUSEUMS OF SCOTLAND, 1992)

Millionaire, the work of one Hulbert Footner and published, ironically, by the Crime Club. From the break in the spine, it would appear that the spy had read 72 pages during his train journey to Edinburgh.

Both Walti and Drugge were taken to MI5's secret interrogation centre, 'Camp 020', at Latchmere House near Kingston upon Thames. There, they were interrogated over the ensuing five months by Lieutenant-Colonel Edward Hinchley-Cooke. Drugge showed no contrition whatsoever and volunteered little of consequence. He did however confirm that Walti had been a member of their group.

Walti on the other hand, while refusing to reveal his real identity, was more loquacious. The essence of the statement he signed on 5 March 1941 was that, prior to the German invasion of Belgium and the low countries, he had utilised his skills as a chauffeur in driving

97

Jews to the French border. He alleged that he had been making as much as 55,000 francs a week from this. At the end of June 1940, after the fall of France, he had met a Norwegian sea captain in an Antwerp caf who had offered to take him to England. His activities had, however, come to the notice of the Gestapo and he was given the choice of working for the Germans or facing a possible death penalty. He stated that he had been duped into going to Norway by ship and, subsequently, onto the plane which took him to Scotland. With regard to the wireless he told Hinchley-Cooke that, 'I had to make sure I didn't lose it and give it to the man at Victoria.' Who the supposed recipient was to have been is not clear.

In spite of its many affecting details, this statement failed to influence the verdict at the trial which was held, in camera, before Mr Justice Asquith at the Old Bailey on 12 and 13 June 1941. Both men were given the only sentence permitted under the Treachery Act, the death penalty. Their appeal was heard, and dismissed, on 21 July. At 0800 hours on Wednesday 6 August Karl Drugge and Robert Petter, for that was Werner Walti's real name, stood up as executioners Albert Pierrepoint and Steve Wade entered his cell.

From the moment she arrived at Holloway Prison from Banff, the case of Vera Erikson is shrouded in mystery. The only certain thing is that she did not stand trial with her accomplices. Willie Merrilees wrote an account of his involvement in the case 25 years later and presumably had it vetted by the Home Office prior to publication. It contains only an oblique reference to Vera's existence, mentioning neither her fate nor even the fact that she was a woman. The official version of events states that she was interned for the duration and released in 1945. Even her real name, variously given as Vera Erikson, Vera von Schalbourg, Vera von Stein and Vera de Cottani-Chalbour, remains a mystery.

The double execution at Wandsworth did not end the Forth Valley's connection with espionage in World War II. Throughout the war, Hitler remained particularly sensitive to threats posed against his forces in Norway. His garrison in that country was bedevilled by both poor communications and an enormously long coastline particularly vulnerable to Allied infiltration. From 1941, Allied deception planners launched a number of operations in an attempt to dupe the German High Command into reinforcing Norway at the expense of other theatres in which offensive operations were planned. The east coast of Scotland and, in particular,

The Portgordon spies were interrogated by Lieutenant-Colonel Edward Hinchley-Cooke. In 1938 Hinchley-Cooke had been responsible for the arrest of Jessie Jordan, a German spy operating in Dundee. (For the full story of Jessie Jordan see This Dangerous Menace - Dundee and the River Tay at War by the same author.)

Hinchley-Cooke's career in the Secret Service had started during the First World War. Being half German on his mother's side, he spoke the language perfectly and acted as a 'stool-pigeon' among German POWs held in British camps.

In the Second World War he was MI5's senior interrogator and a vital part of the Double Cross organisation which 'turned' captured enemy agents.

(AFTER THE BATTLE PUBLICATIONS)

the area around the River Forth played a central role in these deceptions.

Central to the success of these schemes was the use of an expanding network of double agents under the control of MI5's B1a section who would pass back largely false information to Germany. The first of these was Arthur Owens, an anglophobic Welsh engineer whose true loyalties were so suspect that he was placed in Wandsworth Prison on the outbreak of war. From there, under MI5 control, he operated the wireless set given him by Abwehr.

During 1940 and early 1941 this network was enlarged, partly through the 'turning' of captured German agents, and partly by recruiting volunteers. Security was, of course, vital and only those German agents whose capture was not a matter of public knowledge could be used in this way. Sixteen others, including Karl Drugge and Robert Petter, were executed.

It was a vital condition of success that sufficient verifiably true information was passed to the enemy to ensure the agent's credibility. This could only come from the services and, on 2 January 1941, the 'Twenty' Committee was instituted to co-ordinate effort. It was so-called as the Roman numeral for 20 forms a double cross.

Aside from their disinformation and deception role, the double cross agents provided other benefits. Secondary enemy radio signals resulting from agent's information could be intercepted to provide valuable help with codebreaking. A further benefit was that, as Abwehr sent funds across to Britain to support their agents, these fell directly into British hands. They were then used to support operations against Germany.

In December 1941 the Joint Chiefs of Staff approved in principle the first deception operation against Norway under the code name 'Operation Hardboiled'. One of those responsible for planning this operation was Pilot Officer Dennis Wheatley, the novelist. When Wheatley's boss, Oliver Stanley, saw the code word he is said to have enquired, 'Who was the bloody fool who chose such a silly code word?'

Hardboiled involved a notional attack on the Stavanger area by Royal Marines and Polish forces stationed in eastern Scotland. Commandos were trained in mountain warfare, arctic warfare clothing was handed out, Norwegian phrasebooks, currency and maps were issued and the operation was widely gossiped about in Edinburgh and London. Though there is no clear evidence to prove a link with Hardboiled, German forces in Norway were considerably reinforced in April and May 1942. It was a standing joke among servicemen that the issue of desert kit inevitably meant that they were about to be shipped to the far north, and vice-versa.

Operation Torch, the invasion of Vichy French-held North Africa, was due to take place on 8 November 1942. It was the first Anglo-American operation of the war. By this time deception planners were more experienced. In addition, younger, more dynamic staff officers could see the value of deception, not least in saving lives.

One of two major deception plans devised as cover for Torch was Operation Solo One, another threat against Norway. One of the large troop convoys for the Torch landings was assembling in the Clyde and it was put about that this force, which included the Highland Division, was destined for the Narvik and Trondheim areas. Fake radio traffic was initiated around the east of Scotland and a particularly subtle touch was to start a rumour around Scottish ports that Lascar seamen were being offered bonuses to serve above 60 degrees north, something they were not normally obliged to do. Solo One was a success as further reinforcements were sent to Norway in October 1942 and the whole Norwegian Theatre was put on alert as the North African landings took place in November.

Operation Tindall was mounted in October 1943 and was designed to make the enemy believe that five British divisions were about to land in the Stavanger area and move inland as far as Oslo. Dummy aircraft appeared on Scottish airfields such as that on the Duke of Hamilton's estate at Lennoxlove, near Haddington. Vast numbers of tents were erected in the hope that an obliging Luftwaffe pilot would pop over and photograph these entirely bogus invasion preparations.

Earlier, on 7 April 1941, two Norwegians landed from a seaplane at the village of Crovie on the Banffshire coast. They had managed to persuade German Intelligence officers that they were ardent Nazis and that they were prepared to act as spies in Britain.

At Camp 020 they soon established their credentials as double agents and were given the code names Mutt and Jeff. Mutt sent his German controllers detailed and almost entirely fictitious information about Tindall preparations. Included in the flood of information reaching Abwehr were tales that snow chains and anti-freeze were being bought up in large quantities in Scotland.

There was little doubt in German minds that a cross-Channel offensive was about to take place in 1944. Southern Britain was crammed with men and material, and little if anything could be gained from efforts at concealment. As D-Day approached, the object of deception planners was to convince Hitler and his generals that this was not the only operation planned for 1944 and that major offensives were about to be launched in both the Mediterranean and Scandinavia.

Effectively an extension of Operation Tindall, Operation Fortitude North was designed to convince the Germans that an attack near Stavanger in June 1944 would be followed by another in northern Norway to link up with Russian Forces, thus denying German access to the Swedish iron ore fields.

In Fortitude North, MI5 depended heavily on the services of their star agent, Juan Pujol, a Spanish republican code-named Garbo. A dedicated anti-fascist, he had some difficulty in persuading MI5 of his bona-fides. Even before coming under direct MI5 control Pujol had begun to build up a network of wholly fictitious sub-agents and was passing misleading information to Abwehr. One of these imaginary sub-agents was a supposedly wealthy Venezuelan student based in Glasgow, code named Benedict, who had a brother operating from Aberdeen. Benedict was in turn said to be controlling another agent, a Greek communist seaman and deserter, monitoring shipping movements at Methil.

The threat to Norway was centred on the existence of an imaginary British Fourth Army based in Edinburgh and under the command of Lieutenant-General Sir Andrew Thorne, the real General Officer Commanding, Scotland.

Benedict's Greek agent began faithfully reporting on the build-up of an invasion fleet in Methil Roads. To add realism, 71 vessels were moored there in anticipation of an obliging German reconnaissance aircraft coming over to confirm their intelligence.

Also with a major part in the Fortitude North deception was Roman Garby-Czerniawski, a Polish Air Force officer captured by the Germans in France in 1940. Subsequently fooling Abwehr into believing that he was prepared to work for them, he was infiltrated into England where he promptly began to work for MI5 under the code-name Brutus. In April 1944 he radioed his German control with the news that he had seen the insignia of Fourth Army Headquarters in Edinburgh along with other bogus formations at Stirling and Dundee. To add weight to the assertion that the operation in Norway was supposed to link up with Soviet forces, Brutus also reported that a Soviet military mission had attached itself to Fourth Army Headquarters in Edinburgh. Again, a small number of radio vans moving up and down the east coast of Scotland, relaying false signals between these imaginary units, gave the impression of a considerable build-up of forces.

Strategic deception in the Second World War grew into a vast web of inter-connected operations which reached out as far as Japan and the Far East. Hardboiled, Solo One, Tindall and Fortitude North were relatively small but important parts of the overall pattern. Unquestionably, the maintained threat against German forces in Norway saved many Allied lives in North Africa and Europe. The irony is that, by forcing Hitler to maintain a large garrison in Norway, many German lives were saved which would otherwise have ended either at Stalingrad or in Normandy.

'For you, my friends, the war is over!' Home Guards captured by a 'Fifth Columnist' while exercising the defence of Musselburgh in the early morning of Sunday 1 June 1941.
(TRUSTEES OF THE IMPERIAL WAR MUSEUM, LONDON)

Amid tales of derring-do and subterfuge, it is as well to remember that intelligence-gathering in wartime incurred a very real cost in human lives.

When the Special Operations Executive was set up early in the war, it was given a direct order by the Prime Minister that it should, 'Set Europe Ablaze'. Churchill wanted troops trained to mount what he termed 'butcher and bolt' raids on enemy-held territory. Czech, Polish, Danish, French, Dutch, Belgian and Norwegian men and women joined British volunteers in some of the more remote West Highland glens. There they were trained in sabotage, evasion and efficient killing. As SOE expanded, it set up a number of radio listening stations, including one in Belhaven School at Dunbar.

One of the SOE trainees to pass through the GPO Morse Training School in Edinburgh was a young Sunni Muslim woman of Russian extraction, Noor Inayat Khan. Parachuted into France, she operated successfully in the Paris region until betrayed by a French collaborator. After interrogation at the hands of the Gestapo, she was sent to Dachau where she spent her first night in chains. The following morning, 13 September 1944, she was forced to her knees and shot in the back of the head.

Chapter Six

'A Shocking Story Of Ineptitude'

(Admiral Sir Roger Keyes during the Norway debate in the House of Commons 7 May 1940.)

On 23 November 1939 the armed merchant cruiser *Rawalpindi*, a hastily converted P&O liner, was engaged on contraband patrol off south-east Iceland when she was attacked by the German battle-cruisers *Scharnhorst* and *Gniesenau*. It took *Scharnhorst*'s 11-inch guns less than fourteen minutes to pound the old merchantman into a burning wreck. Two hundred and seventy men, including Captain Kennedy, died when she capsized and sank. Only 38 survived, 27 of whom were picked up by the Germans.

Units of the Home Fleet from Rosyth were sent north to hunt for the German warships. Prophetically, the Flag Officer Rosyth, Admiral Ramsay, recorded in his war diary that 'several of our ships are feeling the strain of long passages at high speed in the gales and seas of northern waters. This is not to be marvelled at when one considers the age of some of the ships that are being employed. What really is so marvellous is that the ships have stood up to the strain for so long, a tribute to the ships and the men who man them.'

British naval power had reached its zenith immediately before the First World War. The inter-war years had been characterised by neglect and decline, and many of the ships with which the Royal Navy went to war in 1939 were tarted-up old ladies, long overdue for the scrap heap. For years, scarce resources allocated to the building of new vessels had been misdirected into the building of vulnerable, manpower intensive and expensive battleships which hidebound admirals insisted on seeing as the embodiment of naval might. Hard-won lessons from the First World War that the real need was for fast, effective ships, properly equipped to combat the submarine menace, were almost comprehensively ignored. In addition, senior commanders and politicians alike, failed utterly to comprehend both the vulnerability of capital ships to air attack and the vital role of the aircraft carrier.

As the harsh economic conditions of the thirties forced cuts in the size of the fleet and left no alternative but to modernise pre-First World War Dreadnoughts, Britain's over-extended trade routes to its far flung empire were left hopelessly exposed. This led to the requirement to re-christen old merchant vessels, such as *Rawalpindi*, with the misleadingly resounding title of Armed Merchant Cruiser. Equipped with out- of-date pop guns, with no effective damage control systems or armour protection and crewed by poorly trained reservists, naval pensioners and merchant seamen, they were merely cannon fodder. On 28 October 1939 Winston Churchill wrote, '. . . we are fighting this war with the last war's ships'.

After the *Rawalpindi* incident, *Scharnhorst* and *Gniesenau* slipped past the Home Fleet close to the Norwegian coast and returned to Germany.

The first three months of the war were a period of unrelieved disaster for surface units of the Royal Navy. Twenty-seven merchant vessels had been sunk, along with the battleship *Royal Oak* and the aircraft carrier *Courageous*, and the new cruiser *Belfast* had been seriously damaged by a mine in the Forth. In a mere 13 weeks, 1,300 sailors had been killed.

In stark contrast to the disastrous performance of the surface fleet, the Navy's submarine arm started the war well. Many of its early successes were scored by boats of the Second Flotilla based at Rosyth.

On 14 December 1939 HMS/M *Ursula* scored a torpedo hit on the cruiser *Leipzig* which had earlier been damaged by the Harwich-based boat, HMS/M *Salmon*. As a result of the two attacks, *Leipzig* was out of action for more than a year.

HMS/M *Narwhal* was a large minelayer launched in 1935. On the afternoon of Saturday 17 February she joined the destroyers *Escapade*, *Escort*, *Eclipse* and *Electra* as part of a convoy escort. This unusual role for a submarine was dictated by the desperate shortage of destroyers. Off the Orkney Islands the flotilla handed their charges over to another flotilla and took over a convoy inbound for Methil. They were joined by two more escort destroyers, *Imogen* and *Inglefield*.

At 0755 hours on 24 February CPO Denner, a lookout in *Narwhal*, sighted a U-boat on the surface about five miles astern of the convoy. *Escapade* immediately cracked on speed and raced round to attack but, before she could open fire, the U-boat submerged. *Inglefield, Imogen* and *Escort,* all anxious to be in at the kill, swept round behind *Escapade*. Unfortunately, this caused a near collision and forced *Escapade* to run on away from the target area. The muddle was sorted out and all four destroyers commenced an Asdic sweep, only for the U-boat to surface some distance away and, when fired on, promptly scuttle herself.

Intelligence officers noted that many of the *U 63's* officers were somewhat less than enthusistic about Nazi ideology and that morale amongst the crew was low. Oberleutnant Gunther Lorenz, two of his officers and 20 ratings were landed at Leith three days later by *Imogen* and *Inglefield*.

Narwhal took part in the Norway campaign in her designed role, that of a minelayer. She also carried out two torpedo attacks, sinking one enemy vessel and damaging another. On 22 July she left her new base at Blyth to lay 50 mines off Kristiansund. She was sunk by a Luftwaffe Dornier at 1455 hours the following day.

Following the successful action by British cruisers under Commodore Henry Harwood, the German pocket battleship *Graf Spee* scuttled herself in the mouth of the River Plate, off Uruguay, on 17 December 1939. *Graf Spee*'s foray into the South Atlantic had been made possible by the support of a supply ship, the tanker *Altmark*. When his only customer was destroyed, Captain Dau of the *Altmark* kept his ship in little frequented areas of the South Atlantic for almost two months until he felt confident that the search for him had died down. Then, with 299 prisoners taken from ships sunk by the *Graf Spee* on board, Dau set out to return to Germany by the northern route, skirting the coasts of Greenland, Iceland and Norway.

He had almost succeeded when *Altmark*'s presence in northern waters was first detected on 15 February 1940. Shortly before daybreak the following morning three Hudson aircraft of 224 Squadron, Coastal Command, took off from RAF Leuchars on a long-range search. In bright sunshine near Bergen they first sighted a neutral vessel then, seconds later, the grey hull and upperworks of a tanker. Passing low over the second vessel they identified her as *Altmark*.

By a stroke of luck, Rosyth's Fourth Destroyer Flotilla and the cruiser *Arethusa* were undertaking a sweep in the area. That evening the destroyers *Ivanhoe* and *Intrepid* attempted to make *Altmark* heave to for boarding but she took refuge inside neutral Norwegian territorial waters. She was last seen being escorted into Jøssing Fjord south of Stavanger by two Norwegian gunboats. Captain Philip Vian, commanding the Fourth Flotilla in HMS *Cossack*, attempted to follow only to be himself intercepted by one of the Norwegian gunboats, *Kjell*, whose captain assured Vian that *Altmark* had been searched off Bergen the previous day and that nothing had been found. Unwilling to violate Norwegian neutrality, Vian was left with no alternative but to withdraw and signal the Admiralty for further instructions.

Vian's signal led to the direct intervention of the First Lord of the Admiralty, Winston Churchill. Aware of the possible repercussions which might arise from action by British warships inside Norwegian territorial waters, Churchill consulted with Foreign Secretary, Lord Halifax, before sending Vian the following signal:

'Unless Norwegian torpedo boat undertakes to convoy *Altmark* to Bergen with a joint Anglo-Norwegian guard on board, and a joint escort, you should board *Altmark*, liberate the prisoners and take possession of the ship pending further instructions. If the Norwegian torpedo boat interferes you should warn her to stand off. If she fires on you, you should not reply unless the attack is serious, in which case you should defend yourself using no more force than is necessary, and ceasing fire when she does.'

This was sent at 1525 hours on Friday 16th and, throughout that night, both Churchill and his First Sea Lord, Admiral Sir Dudley Pound, sat up in what was, by his own account, a state of 'some anxiety'.

At 2200 hours *Cossack* entered Jøssing Fjord and, in accordance with his orders, Vian went on board *Kjell*. The Norwegian captain refused a joint escort to Bergen, repeating his assurance that *Altmark* had already been searched and that nothing had been found.

HMS Cossack arrives at Leith carrying 299 men released from the German prison ship Altmark.
(SCOTSMAN NEWSPAPERS LTD)

Vian then informed him of his intention to board the German ship and invited the Norwegian to join him, an offer which was refused.

From his position near the head of the fjord, Captain Dau realised that he was trapped and decided to attempt to break free. As *Cossack* manoeuvred to come alongside, *Altmark* tried to ram her. Dau only succeeded in running his own ship aground by the stern.

A boarding party of two officers and 30 men led by Lieutenant-Commander Turner leapt across onto *Altmark's* deck. Turner made his way to the bridge where he found Dau desperately trying to free his ship and drive the destroyer onto the rocks. As the German crew were being rounded up a single shot injured a British seaman. A brief but fierce fire-fight ensued in which four Germans were killed and five wounded.

Below decks, the boarding party found the British prisoners locked in various store rooms and an empty oil tank. In a final Nelsonian touch, the challenge was made, 'Any Englishmen in there?' When the prisoners cheered, the voice continued, 'Well the Navy's here! Come up out of it.'

By midnight *Cossack* was on her way out of the fjord, past the bemused Norwegian gunboats, and straight to Leith. There she landed her 299 passengers before rejoining the rest of her flotilla,

Sikh, *Nubian*, *Intrepid* and *Ivanhoe*, they having earlier gone on to Rosyth.

As a feat of derring-do, the *Altmark* operation gave a considerable boost to public morale. This had been in steady decline, particularly over news from Finland, where, as Britain and France dithered over sending aid, a massive assault by the Russians, then in alliance with Germany, was overcoming a gallant Finnish army. In Parliament, Chamberlain could take an uncharacteristically resolute and aggressive stand in the face of Norwegian protests over the violation of its territorial waters. Of more lasting importance was the way in which the affair enhanced the status of Winston Churchill.

In Berlin, three days after *Cossack* had berthed at Leith, General Nikolaus von Falkenhorst was received by Adolf Hitler in his study at the Reichs Chancellery. He was ordered to draw up detailed plans for Operation Weserubung, a German invasion of Norway. Speed was of the essence as the *Altmark* affair had convinced Hitler that Britain was preparing to invade Norway and cut off supplies of iron ore vital to his war machine. These were being routed from Sweden, through Norway, to the ice-free port of Narvik and on to Germany by sea.

In London and Paris indecision ruled the day. Conservative MP Harold Macmillan, newly returned from Finland, spoke for an increasing number when he said that, 'The delay, the vacillation, change of front, standing on one foot one day and the other the next before a decision is given - these are patently clear to anyone'. Delays and vacillation continued as Churchill doggedly attempted to gain Cabinet approval for his proposal to mine Norwegian territorial waters, thus blocking the iron ore traffic. After chewing their fingernails over this plan for some weeks, the War Cabinet did eventually give their approval and, on 6 April, four minelayers sailed from Rosyth escorted by the battlecruiser *Renown*, the cruiser *Birmingham* and eight destroyers, all under the command of Admiral Whitworth. At that very moment ships were putting to sea from the German naval base at Wilhelmshaven carrying von Falkenhorst's invasion force.

Some sort of German reaction to the mining was foreseen and also assembling at Rosyth were elements of what was christened Force R4. Four battalions, the 1/5 Royal Leicesters, the 1/4 Royal Lincolnshires, the 1/4 Kings Own Yorkshire Light Infantry and the 1/8 Sherwood Foresters were earmarked to go to Stavanger and

Bergen to forestall any German attempt at a landing. As this small force was loading its equipment into the cruisers *Devonshire, Berwick, York* and *Glasgow,* at 0800 hours on the morning of 7 April, a Coastal Command Hudson spotted a German naval squadron heading north in the Skaggerak. Despite all the warnings of increasing tension in the area, the aircrew failed to report the presence of the enemy ships until they landed at 1100 hours. They thought it was probably only an exercise.

Meanwhile, a number of seemingly innocent German cargo ships were appearing in Norwegian ports. One which failed to reach its destination was the 9,800-ton *Rio de Janeiro,* sunk off Lillesand by the Polish submarine *Orzel* at midday on the 8th. *Orzel* had been operating out of Rosyth since late 1939 when she had succeeded in escaping from internment in Estonia. Lieutenant-Commander Jan Grudzinski gave the *Rio de Janeiro*'s crew five minutes to abandon ship. When the five minutes had elapsed, the German ship was still attempting to escape. Grudzinski fired one torpedo which struck the *Rio de Janeiro* amidships. Immediately hundreds of figures dressed in field grey appeared on her decks. Despite the efforts of Norwegian fishermen, hundreds of German soldiers drowned before they could be rescued.

The element of surprise should have been lost to the invading Germans had not the Norwegian government simply refused to believe the stories of survivors coming ashore in German uniform claiming they were on their way to defend Bergen from British aggression. British Naval Intelligence performed little better. That afternoon the cruisers *Galatea* and *Arethusa* sailed from Rosyth along with a screen of 12 destroyers to intercept what was still thought to be merely a large-scale break-out of commerce raiders.

Having completely outwitted both the Admiralty and a supine Norwegian government, in the early hours of the following morning the Germans were able to gain control of the main cities, ports and airfields in both Norway and Denmark.

British reaction to the invasion was nothing less than shambolic. The Admiralty ordered the four cruisers at Rosyth to 'march troops ashore' as quickly as possible and sail to join the fleet off Norway. Nobody thought fit to inform Sir Charles Forbes, Commander in Chief Home Fleet, that, at a stroke, he had been deprived of the only forces available to him for operations ashore.

Spitfire 'J' of 602 Squadron on patrol over the convoy anchorage in Methil Bay.
Convoys between Methil and Bergen in Norway had begun on 7 November
1939, the last one sailing on 5 April 1940, a mere four days prior to the Ger-
man invasion of that country. Many of the ships in that last convoy were cap-
tured while unloading in Norwegian ports.

Servicing the ports of Leith, Granton and Grangemouth as well as handling
much of the output of the Fife coalfields, Methil grew in importance as an as-
sembly point for the east coast convoys. In doing so it relegated Rosyth to the
purely supportive role that it retains almost 50 years later.

(602 SQUADRON ARCHIVES)

Implicit in the phrase 'march troops ashore' is a sense of orderly disembarkation. Nothing could be further from the truth. The Lincolnshires were exercising on the Rosyth sports field. On returning to the dockyard they found that their kit, stores and weapons had been unceremoniously dumped in a heap on the jetty. The Leicesters were bundled off their ship in less than an hour.

In HMS *York* utter chaos reigned as the 600 Yorkshires struggled desperately to get their stores and equipment ashore while the ship's crew raced against time to prepare her for sea. After an hour of feverish activity, the Yorkshire Territorials stood forlornly on the jetty watching as the cruiser sailed under the Forth Bridge, carrying with her their entire complement of 3-inch mortars and all their signalling equipment. In a few days the battalion would have good cause to bitterly regret the loss of this equipment.

For two days the surface fleet plodded around off the Norwegian coast while the British and French governments tried to make up their minds what to do next. The destroyer *Gurkha*, rescuer of the German airmen shot down off St Abbs Head the previous October, was an early casualty to enemy bombers. The Rosyth submarines, however, soon followed *Orzel* into the thick of the action.

At 1604 hours on 9 April HM S/M *Thistle*, a new 'T' class boat, fired six torpedoes at the *U 4* which was surface running off the entrance to Stavanger Fjord. *U 4*'s crew saw *Thistle*'s torpedoes approaching and managed to take evasive action. At 0113 hours the following morning *Thistle* was charging her batteries on the surface near Utsira when she was herself torpedoed and sunk by the *U 4*.

At 1124 hours on Saturday 20 April HM S/M *Tarpon* was ordered to leave patrol off the Skaggerak and return to Rosyth. She never appeared and only after the war was it possible to discover her fate. As submarines operate in total radio silence, the Rosyth signallers on 20 April would not have known that she had in fact been sunk by a German 'Q' ship ten days earlier. Herbert Caldwell and all his crew were lost.

Meanwhile, *Trident* had sunk the oiler *Posidonia*, *Sunfish* had destroyed the German transports *Amasis* and *Florida*, *Triad* had sunk the transport *Iona*, *Truant* had torpedoed the cruiser *Karlsruhe* and *Triton* had sunk two troop ships, *Friedenau* and *Wigbert* with one salvo of six torpedoes. One particularly sad loss was the gallant Polish *Orzel*. Lieutenant-Commander Grudzinski took his boat on patrol from Rosyth on 23 May and was due to return on 6 June. Nothing more was heard from her.

Further north, at Narvik, two great destroyer battles had been fought and won, aided in the second instance by the decisive intervention of the battleship *Warspite*. Expensive in both ships and men, the victories gained were thrown away. Despite the fact that all German Naval forces in the area had been destroyed and the German garrison in Narvik was last seen to be hastening eastwards, asking for directions to Sweden, it was discovered that there were no troops available to secure the town. As Warspite and her consorts steamed away westwards, Force R4, ideally suited for this task, was still languishing at Rosyth and Dunfermline. Except, that is, for the Yorkshires. They had been loaded into trains at Dunfermline on 11 April and sent to the Clyde. There they were hurriedly embarked on the *Empress of Australia* which promptly sailed north. The only trouble was that all their stores and equipment were still at Rosyth.

At Rosyth things were going from bad to worse for the remaining elements of R4. On 16 April they were being loaded, along with what remained of their equipment, into the trooper *Orion*. Escorted by the cruisers *Galatea* and *Arethusa*, they were to undertake a landing at Namsos.

Meanwhile, a scratch force of 650 seamen and marines from ships refitting at Rosyth had been loaded into four sloops, *Auckland, Black Swan, Flamingo* and *Bittern* which sailed at 0400 hours on the 17th. While sheltering from a gale at Invergordon, this small flotilla of heavily overcrowded ships was diverted to make a landing at Aandalsnes. This they did with considerable success. Someone in Whitehall decided that this force should be reinforced, and that the remnant of R4, currently packing what remained of their precious equipment into *Orion*, were the very men for the job. New orders reached Rosyth just as the loading into *Orion* was being completed. Only then did somebody realise that *Orion* was too large to manoeuvre safely, possibly under air attack, in the narrow fjord off Aandalsnes.

That night, in the blackout, the whole weary and chaotic process of disembarking had to begin again. More equipment was lost and damaged as the exhausted and demoralised men were reloaded into two anti-aircraft cruisers, *Carlisle* and *Curacao*. When these ships sailed, it was discovered that, owing to the lack of space, hundreds

The lessons of Norway, Belgium and France took a long time to sink in. Here, on 2 November 1940, the 3rd Cavalry Training Regiment are being prepared for modern mechanised warfare at Redford Barracks, Edinburgh. Apparently, the Commanding Officer, Colonel Lockett, was a famous international polo player before the war.
(TRUSTEES OF THE IMPERIAL WAR MUSEUM, LONDON)

of men had simply been left on the jetty along with much of the communications equipment, ancillary equipment for anti-aircraft batteries and all the vehicles bar one truck and three motor-cycles.

The inability of the British General Staff to comprehend that, armed with nothing heavier than rifles, this force represented a disaster in the making is simply incomprehensible. Within a week the scantily trained and hopelessly ill-equipped territorials had attacked inland from Aandalsnes only to be just as smartly driven back by the enemy who were equipped with light tanks against which rifles were quite useless. By the 23rd, only nine officers and 300 men remained to be pulled out of the front line.

Arethusa sailed from Rosyth carrying the ground crew of 263 Squadron who were to operate their old Gladiator bi-planes from a frozen lake. Also on board was 50 tons of aviation fuel but, after only two hours at sea, it was discovered that the petrol cans were leaking copiously over the quarterdeck. A single spark, never mind a bomb, would have instantly turned the cruiser into a floating inferno.

Though Aandalsnes was successfully evacuated by the navy on 30 April and 1 May, the war in Norway dragged on until the last troops were evacuated in June 1940. Among those pulled out were the pilots of 263 Squadron who flew their Gladiators aboard the carrier HMS *Glorious* on 7 June. Shortly after 1600 hours the following day, *Glorious* ran into the German battleship *Scharnhorst* and was sunk along with both her attendant destroyers, *Ardent* and *Acasta*. One thousand five hundred and fifteen naval and RAF personnel went down with *Glorious*; only 44 survived. One seaman survived from *Acasta* and two from *Ardent*. Thus, in ignominious defeat, ended the only land campaign of the Second World War to be launched from Scotland. With the end of land operations in Norway, the Navy's great base at Rosyth found itself in the wrong place and increasingly irrelevent as the focus of operations moved out of the North Sea.

As a defeat, Norway was overshadowed by the unceremonious manner in which the British Expeditionary Force was bundled out of France and Belgium that same month. It did, however, bring about the downfall of many of those most directly responsible, not least among whom were Neville Chamberlain and much of the War Cabinet.

Chapter Seven

'Remember Chaps, Bushes Are Not Bulletproof!'

(Instruction to Edinburgh Home Guard on the art of taking cover)

CIVIL DEFENCE

Edinburgh was one of the few cities in Britain to experience the effects of air-raids during the First World War when, on the night of 2/3 April 1916, a Zeppelin airship attacked Leith and Edinburgh, killing 13 and injuring 24. This may well have been a factor in spurring the Corporation into action when, in 1937, the government announced that it was instituting a scheme of Air-Raid Precautions. Early discussions centred on the use of basements and redundant tunnels as air-raid shelters. Among the many locations inspected by the City Engineer in 1938 were the basements of the Usher Hall, the public wash-houses in Henderson's Row, the Harper Memorial Church in Coburg Street, Leith, the Buttercup Dairy in Easter Road and Forsyth's department store in Princes Street. One suggestion was that underground shelters should be constructed close to areas of traffic congestion, such as Princes Street. They could then serve as car parks or a charabanc station, which is much needed.

Much effort was put into the digging of trench shelters in the city's parks, those in Pilrig Park being completed by January 1939. Six trenches were dug in Bruntsfield Terrace, four in Meadowbank Park, two in Barnton Avenue and five in Abercorn Park, Portobello, each being designed to hold 50 people. Promptly neglected, they fell into disrepair. There were a number of incidents where trenches collapsed, including one in the Meadows which resulted in the death of a child. A letter which survives in the Town Clerk's files describes this as having been caused by deplorable official negligence.

There could have been few, if any, of the city's building contractors who failed to spot the opportunities afforded by the enormous programme of building concrete surface shelters. Ford and Torrie Ltd of Hanover Street, understandably unwilling to miss out on the bonanza, went so far as to offer to build at least one free shelter for the Corporation in an effort to convince them of the excellence of their workmanship. But shelter building was by no means always of the highest standard. Six shelters in Dunfermline were among many found to have been shoddily constructed and had to be demolished.

On other occasions the Corporation found itself involved in lengthy disputes with property owners intent on using the desperate shortage of shelter accommodation for their own ends. Late in 1939 the Dunedin Garage in Picardy Place demanded rental of £3 9/- (£3.45) for the use of their basement as a public shelter for local residents. In the face of an almost complete lack of co-operation from the garage, the Corporation abandoned its use as a shelter. Workmen sent along in January 1940 to remove sandbags and other shelter equipment found their way barred unless the Corporation paid up. This particular dispute rumbled on until 1944.

Completed public shelters included the basement of Morrison's Garage at Roseburn Bridge which could hold 100 people. Two hundred could shelter under the YMCA in St Andrew Square and 400 under St Stephen's Church in St Vincent Street.

One ingenious use of existing construction to provide shelter accommodation was the conversion of store rooms under the terrace in the Southern Cemetery. Hitherto used by cemetery staff, these rooms were specially strengthened, had their windows bricked up, new floors and roofs constructed and were provided with ventilation plant.

A more ambitious plan, which got no further than the drawing board, was to dig a deep tunnel shelter from Waverley Bridge to the Grassmarket. This was to have formed part of a complex centred on the existing abandoned railway tunnel which runs from Waverley Market, under Dublin Street and Drummond Place, to Scotland Street. Entrances were to have been provided at Waverley Market, in Queen Street Gardens at the east end of Abercromby Place, and

118

Anderson shelter in an Edinburgh garden.
(EDINBURGH CITY MUSEUMS, THE PEOPLE'S STORY)

at the old goods yard in Scotland Street. In the event, the tunnel was left to the growing of mushrooms.

When the sirens sounded at 1112 hours on 17 October 1939, the day after the Forth raid, all 3,000 employees at the British Rubber Company in Fountainbridge took to the basement for an alert which lasted 18 minutes. A report dated that same day states that a total of 19,095 trench shelters had been dug in Edinburgh and that 6,190 public shelters had been completed under existing buildings. Seven hundred and sixty-eight closes had been provided with blast walls, usually constructed of sandbags. These were to provide secure accommodation for a hopelessly cramped 38,350 shelterers. Thirteen thousand five hundred and thirty-eight corrugated iron 'Anderson' domestic shelters had also been delivered. In total, by October 1939, shelter accommodation was provided in Edinburgh for 140,000 people, around one third of the population.

Later in the war, a small number of 'Morrison' shelters appeared in the city. These were steel cages intended to take the place of a kitchen table. It was soon discovered that many of Edinburgh's buildings were either too old or dilapidated to take their weight.

Towns in Scotland other than Dundee, Rosyth, Glasgow and Edinburgh were not specified to receive government assistance with shelter provision. In Falkirk the town council, whose attitude throughout was to largely ignore the existence of the war, did nothing. In the face of municipal indifference the residents of the town's Oswald Street took matters into their own hands and, in a commendable communal effort, dug their own shelters.

Stirling Town Council made a more concerted effort but came up against a shortage of materials. Due to a lack of corrugated iron and timber for shoring only 300 yards of trenches could be completed. A minimum of 580 yards of trenches would be required to provide cover for 2,300 people, 10 per cent of the town's population. Stirling Town Council also decided that, in view of 'this present emergency', a telephone should be installed in the Town Clerk's house. Dunfermline Town Council, ever conscious of their proximity to Rosyth, had dug trenches in Pittencrieff Park by August 1939.

Some idea of the effectiveness of Edinburgh's blackout can be gained from a statement by Chief Constable Morren in October 1940 when he said that RAF pilots from Turnhouse had told him that, during the hours of darkness, Princes Street looked like Wembley Stadium.

Early official paranoia over the blackout reached the point where it was announced in the *Scotsman* on Saturday, 18 November 1939 that smoking in the open at night could constitute a blackout offence. Any large conurbation like Edinburgh, placed as it is on a river, is relatively easy for a pilot to find, even with a total blackout. Reflected moonlight from canals, rail lines, wet roads and roofs all help in identification. In Falkirk, the town council wrestled with the knotty problem of whether greenhouse roofs should be blacked out. It was decided that the practice should be not encouraged.

For Edwin Seddon, the manager of Edinburgh's Electricity Department, the need for an effective blackout was to provide many headaches. In 1939 he noted that, during the Great War, it had been possible to reduce the intensity of street-lamps until the filaments 'looked like red hairpins in the bulbs'. This was not possible with the new turbo-alternators installed in the inter-war period. The lamps would therefore require to be either unlit or heavily shaded.

During the war, the supply of electricity and gas remained a local authority responsibility. In 1939, Edinburgh Corporation demanded that Seddon have his staff prepare duplicates of all maps and drawings of electricity undertakings within the city. This was to be available should the original set be destroyed. Patiently, Seddon explained that there were 550 such highly detailed drawings and that copying them all would take one draughtsman approximately 13 years. A search for a cheaper and more expeditious method led to the purchase of new equipment from Photostat Ltd at the cost of £336. Meanwhile, the Gas Department was generating much paper, and little else, around a plan to duplicate all their important mains pipes and fit extra valves to those already in place.

The blackout brought with it many hazards. Not a few suffered the pain and indignity of walking straight into trees in the Meadows, others tripped over emergency water pipes laid in the streets to supplement the mains supply for fire-fighting. Road accidents increased sharply despite regular warnings of the danger in the press. The first directly attributable casualty was killed at Buckhaven in Fife less than two weeks into the war. Edinburgh Safety First Council entered into a lengthy wrangle with the police and the city's Transport Department over the brightness of tramcar headlamps.

A series of accidents in 1940 led to a decision to set up lights to illuminate Commercial Street level crossing in Leith while a train was passing over it. Nothing was done for many months as the Dock Commission, the Corporation and the London and North Eastern Railway Company argued over who should pay for the electricity.

Not untypical of the public attitude to ARP was the strongly worded letter of complaint from a Minto Street resident who bemoaned the fact that white lines, painted on the corner of his house to make it visible in the blackout, disfigured the building. He demanded their removal.

At full complement, Edinburgh's Air-Raid Warden service numbered over 7,000 over 80 per cent of whom were men and 85 per cent were volunteers. In April 1940, ARP staff and volunteers in the capital were attempting to hit back at what they termed public ridicule. For them, particularly in the early months of the war, enforcing the blackout was a wholly thankless task. Charles Boog Watson, a leading light in Edinburgh's City Mission, undertook volunteer warden duties near his home in Garscube Terrace. In October 1939 he recorded that one particularly bad blackout offender was the Royal Artillery unit quartered in St George's Church Hall. Another regular offender lived in Succoth Place. The gentleman concerned turned out to be a fellow warden and was dismissed from the service after what Boog Watson describes as a 'warm altercation'.

When the Home Guard was formed in the summer of 1940, large numbers of disgruntled ARP personnel attempted to join up. An impassioned appeal to patriotism by Chief Constable Morren was printed in the Edinburgh ARP Journal in attempt to stem the tide of resignations.

Life as a warden involved men and women being out alone at night and in all weathers, including the winter of 1940-41 when eight to ten degrees of frost was commonplace. In 1943, the Regional Civil Defence Commissioner, Lord Rosebery, reported that it had become increasingly difficult to keep both the public and the civil defence services interested in ARP. To combat boredom 43 discussion leaders had been trained and staff were being employed in making toys. In addition, he noted that the insatiable demands of the forces had reduced the standard of manpower to the point where there were real difficulties in finding men fit enough for work in the Rescue Service.

By far the greatest fear to pervade pre-war planning was that of gas warfare. Gas had been used as a weapon with only partial success by both sides in the Great War. As is so often the case, in times of stress such fears become exaggerated and it was believed that huge enemy airfleets would be able to roam, unmolested, over Britain spreading clouds of deadly toxins behind them. That in 1939 Germany had only a handful of bombers even remotely capable of such a task seems utterly to have failed to penetrate any thinking on the subject. Evidence of the level of fear of this invisible form of warfare can be found in the records of Edinburgh Electricity Department. More than half of its 1,200 staff had been trained in some form of ARP work by the outbreak of war, 60 each in first-aid and fire-fighting and 500 in gas decontamination.

Gas masks were issued, yellow gas detector boards appeared in the streets, and the construction of gas-proof refuge rooms in homes was encouraged. Fife farmers were encouraged to cover stores of grain with oil-dressed tarpaulins to prevent contamination and

The Warden's Dilemma

It is understood a very super course was given recently to A.R.P. Ward Instructors, when everything had to be answered according to the book. Here is a practical exercise for them!

7

Dunfermline Co-op was advertising spectacle frames suitable for use with a gas mask. Government leaflets, the press and the BBC all lectured the public on the need to carry their gas masks at all times but these warnings were widely ignored. 'Gas proof' suits, made from oilskin, were issued to some, but by no means all, ARP personnel. Much annoyance was generated when it was discovered that around 5,000 of these potentially inflammable suits had been packed almost solid into a store room immediately over the main switch gear at McDonald Road electricity sub-station.

South Queensferry had its own gas decontamination squad and a gas cleansing station in Kirkliston Road School. Also at the school was a first-aid post consisting of a reception room, a treatment room and a rest room. Emergency first-aid posts were also set up in the Rio Cinema and the Parish Church Hall. In November 1940 it was decided that a mortuary should be set up at the slaughter house as it was close to both the first-aid post and the cemetery.

Also in late 1940, it was discovered that neither James Scott, South Queensferry's Chief Warden, nor his deputy, David Hinton, possessed a telephone. Apparently, this caused some difficulty when it came to informing them of air-raid alerts.

A side room at the South Queensferry Masonic Lodge was in use as an ARP post. In October 1940, a warden was caught in the Lodge room itself, entertaining his comrades by playing the organ. This considerably displeased Lodge members who were only mollified by the assurance that steps were being taken to ensure that there would be no recurrences of such an offence. Another part of the Masonic Lodge was in use by RAF personnel and the apportionment of bills for services such as electricity and gas was a constant bone of contention. One telephone bill for 10/5d (52p), dating from 1940, was still being argued over in August 1944.

Scotland's cities with their old, densely packed and desperately overcrowded tenement housing represented an enormous fire hazard, made many times worse by the prospect of the threat of high explosive and incendiary bombs. Recruiting for the volunteer Auxiliary Fire Service began early in 1937 and, equipped with trailer pumps, they were soon exercising amid the flames and smoke of fire huts. The London and North Eastern Railway agreed that the Union Canal could be used as a source of water for fire-fighting - but only after the Corporation agreed to pay them 10/- (50p) per annum for the privilege.

RELIABLE EQUIPMENT
for Air Raid Precautions

CORRUGATED STEEL AIR RAID SHELTERS, suitable for erection in garden. To seat 6 persons—size 5 ft. x 4 ft. **£5 10 0**

A.R.P. STIRRUP FIRE PUMP, complete with 30 ft. Hose and dual jet and spray nozzle
EACH - - - - - **29/6**

GALVANISED SAND-CONTAINER, Scoop and Rake with long telescopic handle (made to Home Office Specification.)
THE SET, Complete - - - **25/6**

SANDBAGS, well made from strong jute. **PER DOZEN** - - **8/6**

FLEMING'S
STORES Limited   THE HOUSEHOLD IRONMONGERS

2 & 4 EARL GREY STREET, and
44 HOME STREET (corner of Lochrin Place), EDINBURGH
Also at 259-261 ST. JOHN'S ROAD, CORSTORPHINE

The Corporation's ARP Committee were also concerned over the possible effects of the deluge of water that would arise if the canal bank was breached by a bomb between Sighthill and Leamington Bridge. Three coffer dams were built to reduce the risk to the local population. In Falkirk two 5,000-gallon coffer dams for fire-fighting were constructed in front of the Wheatsheaf Inn in Baxter's Wynd. Mock air-raids also tested the other branches of the ARP service. Rescue parties were being trained by miners in how to burrow safely into a collapsed building, specialised repair parties were being formed along with demolition squads.

Considerable effort was put into devising a system of dealing efficiently with the huge number of dead, injured and homeless expected to result from enemy attack. For the homeless, rest centres

A fire-fighting and decontamination squad at Duncan's Chocolate Factory, Beaverhall Road, Edinburgh.

(EDINBURGH CITY MUSEUMS, THE PEOPLE'S STORY)

Gun Operations Room.
403 Gun Operations Room (8 Anti-Aircraft Group) at Craigiehall, Kirkliston.
(TRUSTEES OF THE IMPERIAL WAR MUSEUM, LONDON)

and communal feeding centres were set up. One of the better known among the latter was the 'Neebor's Tryst' in West Fountainbridge School. For the injured, ambulance depots and dozens of first-aid stations were established throughout Edinburgh, For the dead, 21 church halls were earmarked as mortuaries along with the greyhound racing stadium at Stenhouse.

Linked to the mortuaries were a further 22 information centres run under the auspices of the Council for Social Service. Rather mean-mindedly, and only after a raid in May 1941 had left four dead, did the Corporation agree to the purchase of one Union Jack for each mortuary where they were to be used as palls.

The police stations at Braid Place, Gayfield Square, Torphichen Place, Portobello and Constitution Street in Leith all acted as report centres as did an ARP post in the Cowgate. The bombing of the Caledonian Distillery Bond in Duff Street in September 1940 was the only occasion on which the Casualty Information Service was

Light Anti-Aircraft Unit.
A light anti-aircraft unit, armed with a single Bren-gun, put up an impressive
display in Falkirk in 1939.
(FALKIRK MUSEUMS SERVICE)

required to operate at anything like full stretch. Contemporary records acknowledge that the system was quite overwhelmed.

Lessons were learned, usually from the experience of areas which had come under heavy attack. In April 1941, as a result of experience gained during the Clydebank blitz, the City Social Services Officer was authorised to purchase 87 dozen diapers and a supply of maternity pads. More mundanely, Clydebank had shown that a failure to supply tobacco after air-raids could, according to an official report, 'seriously depress morale'. Civil Defence authorities and the Scottish Tobacco Trades Federation agreed that an emergency supply of 50,000 cigarettes should be kept in Edinburgh, just in case. Group leaders and teams were appointed to rush supplies to bombed areas where they would be sold from a van.

Responsibility for ordering the sounding of the sirens lay with the RAF. The task of actually operating Edinburgh's 53 public sirens was given to the police, whilst the installation and maintenance of the equipment was undertaken by the Post Office Telephones Division, all of which amounted to a recipe for chaos. In extreme weather conditions, sirens simply froze solid, on other occasions electrical faults caused failures. When, on 26 June 1940, the first bombs fell within the city, some sirens sounded the all clear instead of the alert and at least one siren in the Colinton area failed to work at all. Experiments with a talking siren installed on Calton Hill in January 1940 were abandoned after being deemed most unsatisfactory.

On many occasions indecision appears to have gripped those responsible. On 7 July 1940 the alert was sounded at 1400 hours followed a mere two minutes later by the all clear. A further two minutes elapsed before the alert sounded again only for the all clear to sound yet again after another gap of two minutes. The fact was that, all too often, the sound of bombs exploding was followed, almost immediately, by the siren. During a raid on Leith in July 1940, Charles Boog Watson records being awoken, not by the sirens sounding the alert, but by the sound of bombs dropping.

Largely unsung and soon forgotten, the much put upon ARP volunteers were released towards the end of 1944. Paid personnel were unceremoniously dismissed that October.

MILITARY DEFENCES

By nightfall on Monday, 4 September 1939, the day after war was declared, the headquarters of 155 Brigade had been established at Craigiehall outside Edinburgh. Units of the brigade included the 4th and 5th Battalions King's Own Scottish Borderers stationed at Portobello and South Queensferry, the 7/9th Royal Scots at Kinghorn in Fife, 78 Field Regiment Royal Artillery at Burntisland along with 241 (Lowland) Field Company Royal Engineers, and 155 Field Ambulance at Barnton Hotel on the western edge of the city.

Road blocks had been set up north of Aberdour to Kinross and south of Cockenzie to Stobshiel. Defensive positions were being organised to the north of Kinghorn and around both Rosyth and Leith. Six weeks later, the 5th Battalion Black Watch was guarding the Chain Home Low radar station then under construction at Crail and the Transatlantic Wireless Station at Cairngreen, Cupar. The navy's wireless station at Rosyth was in the care of the 9th Battalion Gordon Highlanders and ammunition dumps had been located at Kirkliston and Crossgates in Fife.

Sound Locator Unit.
A sound locator unit west of Edinburgh in 1940. This equipment was designed to detect approaching enemy aircraft from the noise of their engines. Its already limited efficiency would have been considerably impaired by the repeated passes of a threshing machine.

(TRUSTEES OF THE IMPERIAL WAR MUSEUM, LONDON)

Early plans for the defence of the area, though impressive on paper, left rather a lot to be desired in practice. The wiring-in of Turnhouse airfield was not undertaken until October 1939, being completed on the 15th, the day before the Forth raid. Almost two months later it was discovered that the wire had been broken in two places, probably by airmen returning late from the flesh-pots of Kirkliston. Only then does it appear to have occurred to anyone that the fence was not being patrolled at night.

In the event of an enemy force attacking Rosyth and having captured the Forth Bridge, it was decided that the 5th Royal Scots would be ferried across from Port Edgar to reinforce the defence of the dockyard. The fact that these troops, packed into slow-moving craft, would have been in full view of, and direct line of fire of, the same enemy troops whose presence had denied them the use of the bridge seems to have escaped anyone's notice.

On Saturday, 28 October 1939, these troops were placed on their first invasion alert of the war. This was declared in response to reports, emanating from Belgrade, of a supposed German plan for an airborne invasion of the east coast involving a quite fantastic 5,200 aircraft and over 30,000 men. There is little evidence that Winston Churchill, as First Lord of the Admiralty, gave much credit to this absurd report. The following day, however, he wrote that 'every effort should be made to make Rosyth the strongest defended war harbour in the world'.

At the same time the British War Minister, Leslie Hore-Belisha, was proudly announcing to Parliament that 158,000 British troops had been safely despatched to France. In fact, at a total of nine divisions, the British Expeditionary Force was smaller than the Dutch army, less than half the size of the Belgian army and positively tiny by comparison with the French army which stood at 88 divisions. It is a measure of the true level of Britain's lack of preparedness that even this meagre effort denuded the home defences to such a degree that, despite Churchill's stated aim with regard to Rosyth, the defences of the area were largely reduced to a small number of training battalions, latterly the 9th Battalion Fife Home Guard and the static gun batteries dotted around the river. It was soon realised that, surrounded as it was by a ridge of high ground, the dockyard was virtually indefensible. Plans for trenches and fixed defences were not seriously pursued, not least because this would have meant digging up the football pitches on the Navy's recreation ground.

In March 1940 front-line defence of the Lothians was provided by a training battalion of the Royal Scots at Glencorse Barracks and, from Redford Barracks, the 3rd Cavalry Training Regiment mounted, not on tanks, but horses. In reserve were two regiments of medium artillery at Dreghorn and Edinburgh, an artillery training regiment at Aberlady, a signals training regiment at Redford and an officer cadet training unit at Dunbar. Drone Hill radar station was defended by a training company of the King's Own Scottish Borderers.

At 1230 hours on 10 May 1940 the code word 'Julius' was flashed to army units in Scotland. Over seven hours late, it signalled that the war in Europe had begun in earnest with the German invasion of Holland and Belgium. For home defence units there was a desperate shortage of transport. RASC personnel at Leith Fort were ordered to transport the HQ of 28 Brigade from Woodside Hotel in Doune to the coast. In the next few hours an increasingly conflicting series of demands led to their having to hire vehicles from local contractors. The shortage of transport was matched by a shortage of ammunition. When an invasion alert was declared on 21 May 1940 all that could be allocated to units around the Forth was a mere 20 rounds per man. At this time there were only around two dozen field guns in the whole of Scottish Command.

The 21st of May also saw the only offensive action undertaken by the British Expeditionary Force during the Battle of France when two territorial battalions, supported by a small number of tanks and a motor-cycle battalion, attacked German units near Arras. That afternoon Adolf Hitler instructed Admiral Raeder, his naval chief, to prepare detailed plans for a seaborne invasion of Britain. Less than three weeks later the campaign in France ended in bitter recriminations among the Allies and what the new Prime Minister, Winston Churchill, called 'the greatest British military defeat for many centuries'.

Earlier, on 14 May, Churchill's newly appointed War Minister, Anthony Eden, had made a wireless appeal for volunteers for a new national defence force to be called the Local Defence Volunteers. This was not a new idea. Local militias had been levied since time immemorial and a force of Home Defence Volunteers was formed in 1914. Churchill himself had first raised the idea in October 1939.

Around 50 men attended a meeting at Braid Hills Golf Club on the afternoon of Saturday 25 May 1940. The first patrol of what was then B Section of the 4th Company, City of Edinburgh Local Defence Volunteers, reported for duty at 2000 hours the following Wednesday.

The defence of the Braids was co-ordinated through the only convenient telephone; that in the golf clubhouse. With no other form of communication available, those on night patrol used torches to signal to the telephone orderly who sat beside an open window in the clubhouse. The flashing lights had many nervous local residents quite convinced that the trilby-hatted and trench-coated defenders of Morningside were, in reality, advance parties of Hitler's legions.

That should fool 'em! Pillbox outside the Rutland Hotel in Shandwick Place Edinburgh in August 1940.
Edinburgh Corporation even went so far as to camouflage the roofs of their buses. The practical value of camouflage applied to a bus proceeding along Lothian Road does not appear to have been considered.

(TRUSTEES OF THE IMPERIAL WAR MUSEUM, LONDON)

At first there were next to no weapons or ammunition, no uniforms, no money and no organisation. On being formed, A Company of the 8th Battalion, Edinburgh Home Guard, trained with old wooden rifles someone had found in Portobello. Their only functional weapons were ten-muzzle loading rifles normally used by Edinburgh Academy for target practice, one Boer War vintage Mauser rifle and the commanding officer's revolver. The 7th Battalion, Fife Home Guard boasted a miscellaneous collection of pistols which, by their own admission, would have been deadlier had they possessed any ammunition for them.

It must be said that Scottish Command records show little real fear of an actual invasion. In the event of an invasion of England, the issue would have been decided long before the Panzers reached

Carter Bar. Nevertheless, during the summer of 1940, feverish anti-invasion preparations were undertaken. Wide open spaces were regarded with great concern lest they provide suitable landing grounds for aircraft or gliders. Under a programme oddly titled 'The Immobilisation of Golf Courses', obstacles were scattered over Scotland's hallowed fairways. These included old cars, barrels filled with earth, drain pipes, sections of brick wall and even sheep. Bruntsfield Links sprouted poles, Craigentinny and Craigieknowe golf courses were trenched and banked and the Cramond course was liberally spread with railway sleepers.

South of the Forth a defensive line of strongpoints was established along the River Esk. This was in fact the northernmost end of a line of fortifications, known as the GHQ Line, which ran from the Thames to East Lothian. In Fife, every mechanical digger in Scotland, about 170 in all, along with a large number of locally recruited volunteers were employed on the digging of an anti-tank ditch which ran right across the county from Kirkcaldy, through Markinch and Ladybank, to Newburgh on the south bank of the Tay. Clearly, the scenic East Neuk was to be abandoned to the enemy while the coalfields of West Fife were to be defended to the last.

Despite concerns expressed about possible disfigurement of the area, defensive positions were set up in the Meadows. Slit trenches were dug at both ends of Middle Meadow Walk although falling into the trench at the corner of Argyle Place in the blackout was an ever-present hazard. Further digging was carried out at Inverleith Park, Leith Links and Crewe Toll. In 1941, the Corporation was informed that 'it was necessary' for D Company of the 6th Battalion to dig slit trenches in gardens at Johnston Terrace, Castle Terrace and King's Stables Road.

Before the war a whole range of what were termed 'Vulnerable Points' had been identified. These VPs, as they were known, included Drem Airfield (VP 331), Turnhouse Airfield (VP 320), Drone Hill radar station (VP304) and, for some reason, the East Manse at Linlithgow (VP 343). Other VPs included all the Forth Fixed Defences, the Forth Bridge, the airfields at Crail and Donibristle and the various harbours such as Leith, Granton, Rosyth and Methil. An enormous number of blockhouses were constructed to defend these and other locations. The fact that this was done with scant regard for the safety of road users is clear from a survey conducted by Edinburgh police in 1942. Many of them had the effect of creating blind corners on busy main roads, particularly hazardous in the blackout. One blockhouse in Colinton Road, outside Redford Barracks, was held directly responsible for an accident which killed two and injured four. By the time of the police survey 155 accidents attributable to the presence of blockhouses had taken place in which 55 people had been injured. At least 40 such accidents had taken place at the corner of Lothian Road and Princes Street, injuring 17. Despite this, and with invasion not even a remote possibility, as late as 1943 the military were most reluctant to sanction the removal of many of these hazards. For some unspecified reason, early in 1944, the army sought permission to erect even more pillboxes in the city.

Another hazard for wartime road users was the roadblock, literally hundreds of which sprang up across south-east Scotland during 1940. It did not take long to discover that, whilst unlikely to hinder an attacking enemy, these obstructions caused great difficulty for heavy lorries, in particular RAF aircraft transporters. A particular nuisance for traffic leaving the docks was the road-block outside Leith Central Station.

Those manning one roadblock on the edge of Edinburgh had to wait for a blacksmith's forge to cool down before mounting their machine-gun. Another, and perhaps one of the better known, was that at Hillend on the main A 702 road south to Biggar. It was built, in June 1940, on a site described by Lieutenant White, the platoon commander responsible for its defence, as 'rich in defects'. Immediately in front of the roadblock was a blind summit and covering fire was provided from a pillbox built on, of all things, a petrol station. The barricade across the road was made up of two concrete breastworks with gaps echeloned to allow vehicles to pass through. These gaps could be closed by rolling concrete 'cheeses' into position with crowbars.

The desperate shortage of anti-tank weapons forced those concerned to look for alternatives, one of which was the 'flame trap', a pool of burning oil in which the tank and its crew were supposed to be incinerated. At Hillend, a large reservoir was constructed among the trees on the rising ground west of the road and pipes were laid along either side of the road in front of the roadblock. Under gravity, controlled by a man operating a valve located in a slit trench under the hedge at the roadside, oil would spray out of perforations in these pipes and onto the road surface. This same

*General Andrew Thorne, General Officer Commanding, Scottish Command,
discussing the use of a bow, and arrows tipped with fireworks, with members of
165 Officer Cadet Training Unit during an exercise in Musselburgh in June
1941. This unlikely weapon was being used to simulate bombs exploding
among Home Guard Units on the opposite bank of the River Esk.*
(TRUSTEES OF THE IMPERIAL WAR MUSEUM, LONDON)

man also had the unenviable task of igniting the oil with a Molotov
cocktail. This, it was acknowledged, placed him in direct line of fire
of both the enemy and his fellow Home Guardsmen.

No sooner had the installation of this fearsome device been completed than a demonstration was arranged. The valve was opened, the road sprayed with oil and a Molotov cocktail was thrown onto it. Observers were instantly rewarded with a lurid sheet of flame and clouds of black smoke. Looks of satisfaction changed to embarrassed concern when it was noticed that the flames had spread to the hedge and that a telegraph pole carrying the main trunk lines was well alight. The fire brigade dealt efficiently with the blaze before too much damage was done.

Inchkeith Battery during a practice shoot by the Home Guard in 1943.
Shortly after 0930 hours on 21 February 1940 the Admiralty trawler Peter Carey strayed out of the swept channel south of Inchkeith and was in danger of striking a mine. The Battery Commander on Inchkeith attempted to warn the trawler by firing a 6-inch practice round across his bows. Having had the desired effect on the trawler, the round ricochetted off the surface of the water and carried on for another three-and-a-half miles. It passed through Neptune Mills in Leith and hurtled across the road into 118 Salamander Street. There it wrecked the interior of a flat and destroyed a garden shed before coming to rest against an air-raid shelter. Mrs Cairns was in her flat at the time but escaped with a scalp wound. Her two children were unharmed.
It is said that the shell, was returned to Inchkeith with a note attached which stated, simply, 'We believe this belongs to you.'
(TRUSTEES OF THE IMPERIAL WAR MUSEUM, LONDON)

137

Other, perhaps more conventional, weapons had begun to arrive by the end of 1940. Muzzle-loading target rifles were replaced with Lewis guns. Northover projectors which could fire a Molotov cocktail or a grenade had been issued as had Spigot mortars, Mills bombs and a large consignment of First World War American rifles. When A company of the 8th Battalion received their Thompson sub-machine-gun it immediately became 'the exhibition piece' in their armoury. Later Sten guns became the standard issue weapon for Home Guard units.

With these weapons came increasing quantities of ammunition until, in August 1943, it was estimated that Home Guard units in the Lothians and Peeblesshire were holding almost 500,000 rounds of small arms ammunition. This turned out to be a serious under-estimate. Initial arrangements for the storage of ammunition had been hasty to say the least and an inspection carried out in 1943 revealed a horrifying picture of dangerous neglect.

Fifteen thousand small arms rounds were stored, along with nearly 1,500 grenades and mortar bombs in a hut in George Heriot's grounds and 34,000 small arms rounds were being kept in a hut at the back of the Royal Dick Veterinary College along with 1,900 grenades. These appear to have been kept properly ventilated and in good condition, but worse was to come.

At 30 Rutland Square, the HQ of E company of the 8th Battalion, 2,000 rounds of small arms ammunition and 300 grenades were stored in the house for lack of any other accommodation. 'E' company also had 12,000 rounds and over 300 rifle grenades stored in a wine cellar in the basement of a residential block at 4 Oxford Terrace.

Worst of all was the discovery made in the basement of 8th Battalion HQ at 1 Grosvenor Gardens. Here, again in a residential block, 210,000 small arms rounds were found along with 4,582 grenades. According to Captain Gray of 105 Command Ammunition Depot RAOC, much of this was in bad condition owing to poor storage and was 'in fact dangerous'. It was hastily moved away to a hut at Murrayfield. Nobody dared to speculate on the possible effects had an enemy bomb landed anywhere near one of these magazines.

Though training was still sketchy, by early 1941 the worst of the early improvisations had given way to a greater degree of profes-sionalism. The first steps towards the creation of a citizen army had

With great care, sappers examine every stick of furniture in the newly liberated 'Estaminet des trois Roses' (prop. Mme Dubois) for hidden booby traps.

In reality this was a three-sided army hut set up in Liberton, Edinburgh, to train engineers in mine and booby trap clearance. However, the entirely fictional Mme Dubois set very high standards of behaviour. At the entrance to her establishment she had painted the warning, 'Defense de uriner'.

A familiar sight in photographs of mine clearance operations following D-Day was the electronic mine detector developed at the Polish Engineering Cadet School in Tay Street, Dundee.

Thousands of troops were stationed all over south-east Scotland as they prepared for the assault on Hitler's 'Festung Europa' in June 1944. Royal Marines used converted Thames barges for assault training at Gullane beach and anti-aircraft units exercised at Gosford House near Longniddry. At Leven in Fife the Polish Airborne Brigade under General Sosabowski involved target practice at Dreghorn with borrowed rifles and the few rounds that could be spared. Soon, however, the ranges at Redford and Hailes Quarry were being peppered with mortar bombs and Molotov cocktails. At Castlelaw Gas Compounds new recruits stumbled around, coughing and spluttering as they learned the rudiments of anti-gas warfare. Signalling and despatch riders courses were under way at Redford Barracks and, on Sunday afternoons at the Rutland Cinema, such gems as *Ten Tips for Tackling Tanks* were required viewing. Regular lectures at the Royal Arch Halls in Queen Street and George Heriot's School covered such diverse topics as first aid, map reading, signalling and field-craft, and many attended the Scottish Command Camouflage School at Ravelston Elms. As the tide of war swung in favour of the Allies, this training increasingly took the form of preparation for service in the regular forces. A number of men attended courses at the Commando Training Centre near Spean Bridge.

Home Guardsmen, as a largely static force, were encouraged to know their immediate area of operations intimately. They learned to pass, unseen, through railway tunnels, factories, basements, backcourts and gardens. Street fighting was taught at Couper Street in Leith and on the site of the bombed out bonded store in Duff Street. This involved what was described as 'hectic steeplechasing' through houses without stairs or floors and over garden walls garlanded with barbed wire.

Regular exercises and demonstrations were held which provided considerable entertainment for participants and observers alike. One demonstration at Cambo in Fife was enlivened by the sight and sound of an old First World War Rolls Royce armoured car which

made many friends among the local population. In September 1944 they were dropped into Holland as part of the ill-fated Arnhem operation.

Feeding and clothing thousands of men and women proved a considerable headache for the RASC Central Supply Depot at Murrayfield. Here essential items were stored including foot powder and ascorbic acid tablets, the latter no doubt to relieve the after effects of delicacies such as herrings in tomato sauce, tinned potatoes, pilchards and margarine. Also part of the Murrayfield inventory were thousands of gallons of rum and millions of cigarettes.

After D-Day the former army camps were given a new role as POW camps, most notably at Stobs near Hawick. Other POW camps were set up at Castle Rankine near Denny in Stirlingshire, at Gosford House, at Dalkeith, Kirknewton and Ladybank in Fife.

(TRUSTEES OF THE IMPERIAL WAR MUSEUM, LONDON)

had been unearthed on Crail airfield by members of the St Andrews University OTC.

With bloodthirsty orders to 'Kill the enemy - No prisoners to be taken!' ringing in their ears, small groups of men charged up the southern slopes of Arthur's Seat. Meanwhile, angry farmers were to be seen collecting livestock which had wandered off after Home Guardsmen had left gates open. When their protests fell on deaf ears the farmers erected obstacles in front of the gates only to find that these had been broken down and the gates again left open. Complaints also came in from members of the public left weeping after Guardsmen picked up the wrong canisters, releasing tear gas instead of smoke screen.

Exercise 'Peggy' in February 1942 was designed to test the defences of the Hillend and Penicuik districts which were to be defended by, amongst others, the 3rd Battalion City of Edinburgh Home Guard and the Midlothian battalion. The enemy was represented by the 52nd Reconnaissance Corps and it was decided that they had won convincingly, in spite of most of their vehicles having suffered 'stoppages due to ice'. Exercise 'Badger' lasted 48 hours amid heavy snow and tested the defences of Leith Docks and Cramond. On one of the many exercises held around the capital, one platoon found that it was running short of ammunition. Showing commendable resource, they resorted to using peeled potatoes which they carefully retrieved for the following day's dinner.

During an exercise on Braid Hills one enthusiastic platoon commander was seen exhorting his men to attack with his back to the enemy, blissfully unaware of the 'enemy' machine-gun post immediately to his rear. Another Home Guardsman delighted his colleagues during Exercise 'Bruce' in June 1941 by insisting on having his usual bath and breakfast before reporting for a 'stand-to'.

As with the civil defence services, it became more and more difficult to maintain morale and enthusiasm in the ranks of the Home Guard. Efforts to keep enthusiasm alive included boxing matches at the Eldorado in Leith, parades, summer camps and social events.

The Lauriston battalion organised children's Christmas parties where games such as 'The Grand Old Duke of York', 'Farmer in the Den', 'Flip the Kipper' and 'Sticking the Tail on the Donkey' proved great favourites. Another idea was the institution of 'Community Dancing Classes' in an effort to keep up morale and introduce the young to folk dances from England, Scotland and Scandinavia which they regard as absurd and old-fashioned. Little enthusiasm appears to have greeted this suggestion.

For the last time, on a raw afternoon at the beginning of December 1944, so very different from the warm days of May 1940, the order, 'Fall out the Officers, Company Dismiss', was given. A few days later, at the stand-down dinner of the 8th Battalion, their Commanding Officer, Lieutenant-Colonel A. C. Murray, closed his speech with these lines from Hiawatha:

All your strength is in your union,
All your danger is in discord.

One of his officers put it another way when he wrote:

With prehistoric weapons, sharpened pikes and even sticks,
(Well, you've got to grip on something when you're in a bloody fix)
They ranged the moor and valley, mounted sentry through the night
In much appalling weather, but they found no foe to fight.

Chapter Eight

Quenched the Violence of Fire

On the afternoon of Tuesday, 8 May 1945, the Church of the Holy Rude in Stirling was packed for a Service of Thanksgiving. In the pulpit was the Rev. Lewis Sutherland who combined his duties at Stirling with that of padre to 602 Squadron. Many of his congregation were deeply affected by the lesson (Hebrews XI 32-40), which speaks of the prophets:

> 33 *Who through faith subdued kingdoms, wrought righteousness, obtained promises, stopped the mouths of lions,*
> 34 *Quenched the violence of fire, escaped the edge of the sword, out of weakness were made strong, waxed valiant in the fight, turned to fight the armies of the aliens.*

The service ended with the rousing hymn, *O God, Our Help in Ages Past*. That night the band of Queen Victoria School, Dunblane, played for dancers in King's Park, the streets of the town were decorated and the Black Boy Fountain was floodlit. It was VE Day, the war in Europe was over. Scenes of wild rejoicing had, in fact, begun the previous evening with bonfires being lit and crowds taking to the streets, though at Broomhall in Fife, the Earl of Elgin was instructed not to light a victory bonfire on the estate as a U-boat had just sunk two ships off May Island.

King George VI spoke to the country on VE night. 'There is great comfort,' he said, 'in the thought that the years of darkness and danger in which the children of our country have grown up are over and, please God, for ever. We shall have failed, and the blood of our dearest shall have flowed in vain, if the victory which they died to win does not lead to a lasting peace. To that then let us turn our thoughts on this day of just triumph and proud sorrow . . .'

The King's heartfelt plea eloquently expressed the mixed feelings of most on that day of victory. There was great happiness and relief that the war was over but there was also an acute awareness of what it had all cost.

Throughout the war, the government had gone to great lengths to assess public opinion and morale. Researchers, employed by the Ministry of Information were better known as 'Cooper's Snoopers' after the Minister, Duff Cooper. In Edinburgh, 150 examiners were reading 14,000 letters every week. What these and other surveys reveal is that public opinion in Scotland was by no means solidly in favour of the war, particularly in its early months.

The Communist Party in Scotland were initially in favour of the war as being anti-fascist. After the Soviet Union, in alliance with Germany, invaded Poland and Finland, the party was forced into a cynical volte-face. Slavishly following the line dictated by Moscow, they described the war as capitalist, imperialist aggression by Britain and France.

Throughout this period the steady increase in Communist Party membership in Scotland was reflected in increased sales of the *Daily Worker*. Communist MP Willie Gallacher and Councillor Abe Moffat were addressing well-attended anti-war meetings in Fife. In Dunfermline and Leslie they could attract 400 people, in Kincardine, Lochore and Kelty, audiences of up to 200. Two thousand four hundred people attended a Communist Party rally addressed by Willie Gallacher and Communist Party General Secretary Harry Pollitt in Edinburgh on 29 April 1940. Despite the party's craven servility towards the Moscow line many individual members, Gallacher and Pollitt included, held pro-war views which they were forced to suppress in the name of party unity until Germany invaded the Soviet Union on 22 June 1941. Overnight, the party line changed again and the war was no longer 'imperialist'. The pent-up feelings of many influential party members came out in vociferous calls for a second front to aid Soviet armies reeling under the German onslaught.

Public opinion only really began to harden in favour of the war as the spectre of defeat in Europe loomed and the war came very much closer to home. Until then strong anti-war sentiments had

Women and children from Middlefield, Falkirk, collecting for the Spitfire Fund. Wartime travel was severely restricted and activities like this provided a much needed diversion for 'stay-at-home' holidaymakers. The 'Falkirk Bairn' Spitfire was lost to ground fire over Europe in 1944 after accounting for two enemy fighters.
The South Queensferry and Dalmeny Savings Committee raised ú16,850 to 'purchase' their own Spitfire. Taken on charge by 111 Squadron on 6 April 1944, it was flown by Flight-Lieutenant Livingston during operations around Anzio in Italy. It crashed three weeks later, on 22 April.
(FALKIRK MUSEUMS SERVICE)

also been expressed by the Peace Pledge Union and the Women's Peace Movement. Following the German invasion of Norway in April 1940, the Ministry of Home Security reported that attendances at their meetings on the Mound were 'as large as ever'.

That a disaster was taking place in Europe first became apparent to the public on 16 May. This came as a severe shock to a nation brought up to believe in the invincibility of British imperial power. Ministry of Information researchers in Edinburgh reported that people were becoming 'more depressed by the day'. By 24 May 1940 it was reported that there was 'less enthusiasm for Communist

Party meetings by the day'. The arrests of Mosley, Ramsay and other fascists were particularly well received.

The 'widespread tension and apprehension' reported the following week had many side-effects. One was the persecution of Scotland's Italian minority. What the Ministry of Home Security termed 'a certain amount of sporadic rioting' began towards the end of May. Over the next two weeks hundreds of Italian-owned shops were ransacked in what the Edinburgh *Evening News* described as an 'Orgy of Window-Breaking and Looting'. Shops in Leith were wrecked and Notarangelo's in Manor Street, Falkirk, was looted by an angry crowd.

Matters came to a head after Mussolini brought Italy into the war on 10 June 1940. All over Scotland, thousands of Italians were rounded up and interned prior to being deported. Many were drowned when the liner *Arandora Star* was torpedoed while taking German and Italian internees to Canada.

Alien baiting did not stop at the Italians. Early in June 1940 Ministry of Information researchers were concerned by an upsurge in anti-semitism in Edinburgh.

Particularly strong among the received images of wartime Britain is that of the family gathered round the wireless, enthralled and inspired by the speeches of Winston Churchill. 'We shall fight them on the beaches . . ., we shall never surrender'. The legend continues that, throughout the war, the BBC unfailingly provided entertainment of the highest quality and a news service unfettered by government control. That at least is the myth.

The reality was very different. All but the lightest of the BBC's output was subject to rigid government control and staff were carefully vetted by MI5. A Christmas broadcast in December 1940 by the Glasgow Orpheus Choir was cancelled as its musical director, Sir Hugh Roberton, was a pacifist.

Complaints about the blandness of BBC output began immediately on the outbreak of war. Criticism mounted during 1940 with references to BBC output being 'puerile and pitiable'. One critic even dismissed the BBC as having 'moral rickets'. Much of the entertainment output was banal, stuffy and written for an English audience, the Scottish Regional Service having closed down the day before war broke out. News bulletins were little more than relays of official announcements passed on without comment or amplification.

Silly slogans, delivered with starchy, high-minded dignity, did little to improve matters. In May 1941 Germany was undisputed master of Europe. Yet a broadcast that month contained the assertion that 'the myth of German might is very much moth-eaten'. Ministry of Information surveys show that few were taken in by this sort of nonsense.

Neither the 'fight them on the beaches' speech, nor the equally famous 'This was their finest hour' speech, were broadcast by Churchill himself. They were read by Norman Shelley, an actor with a talent for mimic, better known for playing Larry the Lamb on Children's Hour.

Listening to enemy broadcasts was reported as on the increase in Scotland during May 1940. In particular, it was said that 'enemy broadcasts are listened to keenly' in, of all places, Bo'ness. Two enemy radio stations were beamed to Scotland. Radio Caledonia carried propaganda intended to inflame nationalist sentiments. Star of the New British Broadcasting Station was former Right Club member, William Joyce, otherwise known as Lord Haw-Haw due to his nasal tones. It was officially acknowledged that rumours started by those listening to Lord Haw-Haw carried considerable weight in Scotland.

A rumour doing the rounds in June 1940 had many believing that motorcycles with full petrol tanks had been secreted along the east coast for use by enemy parachutists. Others spoke of shadowy figures seen carrying out sabotage in Leith Docks, mysterious flashing lights attracting enemy bombers and 'hairy-handed nuns' wandering the Lothians. One Leith child was told not to eat sweets he found lying in the street as the Germans were dropping poisoned boilings all over Scotland!

Hysteria reached such levels that there was widespread support for a move, in Edinburgh, to form a so-called Sixth Column to root out Fifth Columnists. Edinburgh police were said to be 'unhappy' at the prospect of vigilante groups roaming the streets.

The propaganda machine convinced the majority of the 'perfidy' of Belgian King Leopold for surrendering before the British Expeditionary Force could run away. This despite the fact that British commanders had been careful not to tell their Belgian counterparts that the BEF was abandoning them to their fate. The French surrender was treated as 'treachery'. Not made public was the fact

'Tittle Tattle Cost the Battle'
(EDINBURGH CITY MUSEUMS, THE PEOPLE'S STORY)

that the evacuation from Dunkirk was largely made possible by a valiant rearguard action fought by the French army.

The effortless manner in which the Japanese army overran British and Dutch interests in the Far East brought spirits to a particularly low ebb. This was followed, in June 1942, by the fall of Tobruk which, according to Lord Rosebery, was greeted in eastern Scotland 'with dismay'. The bleak nature of even the strictly censored news given out was too much for some, particularly those with relatives serving overseas. They simply stopped reading newspapers and listening to the wireless.

Part of the mythology surrounding Scotland's war centres on a workforce with its shoulder to the wheel, united in the drive for increased production. Again, this is only partially true. In the first two weeks of April 1940 300 men were on strike at Henry Robb's in Leith over the conduct of a supervisor. Eighty men were out that week at Niddrie Brickworks and 248 men at Grangemouth Docks went on strike over the employment of non-union labour. To the great disgust of many, particularly servicemen, as the country faced the threat of imminent invasion in June, Fife miners refused to forego their annual holidays. Industrial relations did improve but tiredness and irritability had set in by September 1940. In November 500 Bannockburn miners came out for better wages despite the fact that, under Order 1305, strikes had been forbidden.

Despite these early problems, war production did settle down. Factories in Falkirk made tank parts, Mills bombs, 25-pounder shells and incendiaries. Thirty-seven ships were built in Grangemouth and many more repaired. Also in Grangemouth, immediately prior to D-Day, Christie and Vesey's sawmill was jammed with Bailey Bridge sections, temporary airstrip materials and pipelines. Henry Robb's at Leith built 42 naval vessels and 14 merchant ships. They also repaired and refitted almost 3,000 others. Among the ships built at Leith were headquarters vessels used in the D-Day landings and specialised pipelayers used in the laying of PLUTO, the pipeline under the ocean which supplied fuel for the allied armies in Europe. In Edinburgh, Ferranti's produced top secret gyro gunsights and the Fountainbridge Rubber Mill turned out thousands of service respirators, carburettor diaphragms and aircraft mouldings.

Allied victory at El Alamein and Stalingrad's resistance at the end of 1942 aroused 'admiring wonder' in Scotland. By 1943 American soldiers were to be seen in large numbers in Edinburgh. Young female voices could be heard shouting, 'Have you got any gum, chum', to GIs at the windows of the Mount Royal Hotel. Relationships were not always cordial. Many young GIs hid their homesickness behind a mask of arrogance and fights between Americans and Scots in the capital's dance halls were commonplace. In addition, the segregation of black GIs brought home the realities of racism to many Scots for the first time.

There were many Edinburgh children who found that their pals had new brothers or sisters even though their fathers had not been home for two years. Meanwhile, the *Falkirk Herald* was full of praise for that rather staider town's 'War-celibate housewives' who were to be seen queuing for food.

The first prisoners of war to arrive in Scotland in any numbers were Italians captured in North Africa. They were followed by thousands of Germans taken prisoner in Europe after D-Day. Former army camps were turned into POW camps, most notably at Stobs near Hawick. POW camps also existed at Dalkeith, at Gosford House near Longniddry, at Castle Rankine near Denny in Stirlingshire, at Kirknewton and at Ladybank in Fife. These Italians seen with locals near Duns probably came from a camp at Chirnside.

(HUNTLY HOUSE)

The years of defeat and despair were a thing of the past. Victory was now assured.

603 (City of Edinburgh) Squadron brought its Spitfire XVIs back to RAF Turnhouse on 28 April 1945. The squadron had given distinguished service in the defence of Malta during 1942. It had then been re-equipped with Beaufighters as an anti-shipping strike unit in North Africa before returning to Europe as a fighter unit early in 1945. Of the pre-war auxiliary personnel only about 30 ground crew remained with the squadron.

On 4 May 1945 the squadron's officers made a swift sortie into Edinburgh, returning via the WAAF officers' mess. The following day, in poor weather, Flight-Lieutenant Batchelor led 12 Spitfires on a display of formation flying over the city.

The squadron moved to Drem on 7 May and that day's entry in its Operational Record Book concludes thus: 'Apparently the War is over.'

Bibliography

PUBLISHED WORKS
The Myth of the Blitz, Angus Calder. Jonathan Cape 1991.
1940 - Myth and Reality, Clive Ponting. Hamish Hamilton 1990.
Conspirator, Ray Bearse and Anthony Read, MacMillan 1991.
The Man who was 'M', Anthony Masters. Blackwell 1984.
Against the Tide, Katharine Atholl 1874-1960, S. J. Hetherington. Aberdeen University Press 1989.
The Nameless War, A. H. Maule Ramsay. Britons Publishing Society 1952.
Ten Days that Saved the West, John Costello. Bantam Press 1991.
Fellow Travellers of the Right, Prof. Richard Griffiths. Constable 1980.
British Intelligence in the Second World War, Vol. IV Security and Counter Intelligence, F. H. Hinsley and C. A. G. Simkins. HMSO 1990.
Some were Spies, the Earl Jowitt. Hodder and Stoughton 1954.
One Girl's War, Joan Miller. Brandon 1986.
MI5, Nigel West. Bodley Head 1981.
The Short Arm of the Law, William Merrilees OBE. John Long 1966.
Strategic Deception in the Second World War, Prof. Michael Howard CBE. Pimlico 1992. (Originally published as vol. V of *British Intelligence in the Second World War*. HMSO 1990.)
The Deception Planners, Dennis Wheatley. Hutchinson 1980
Action Stations 7, David Smith. Patrick Stephens 1983.
Spitfire into War, Air Vice Marshal Sandy Johnstone CB DFC. William Kimber 1986.

Lions Rampant, Douglas McRoberts. William Kimber 1985.
The Rise and Fall of the German Air Force. Official Report reprinted by Arms and Armour Press 1983.
The Luftwaffe War Diaries, Cajus Bekker. Corgi 1969.
Glasgow's Own, 602 (City of Glasgow) Squadron, Dugald Cameron. Squadron Prints 1987.
The Battle of Britain Then and Now, ed. Winston Ramsey. After the Battle Publications 1980.
The Blitz Then and Now, vols I to III, ed. Winston Ramsey. After the Battle Publications 1989.
Submarines Versus U-Boats, Geoffrey Jones. William Kimber 1986.
Beneath the Waves, A History of H.M. Submarine Losses, A.S. Evans. William Kimber 1986.
Norway 1940, Francois Kersaudy. Collins 1990.
A Prologue to War, *The Navy's Part in the Narvik Campaign*, Ewart Brookes. Jarrolds 1966.
Finest Hour - Winston Spencer Churchill 1939-1941, Martin Gilbert. William Heinemann 1983.
Most Secret War, Prof. R.V. Jones. Hamish Hamilton 1978.
Lauriston 1940-44, *History of 'A' Company of the Eighth Battalion, City of Edinburgh Home Guard*. Captain Andrew J. Fiskin. Livingstone & Co. 1945.
The Watch on the Braids, *The Record of an Edinburgh Home Guard Company 1940-1945*, Various. Private publication.
1945 - The World We Fought For, Robert Kee. Hamish Hamilton 1985.

Newspapers And Periodicals
The *Times* 1938-1940.
The *Scotsman* 1938-1945.
The Edinburgh *Evening News* 1939-1945.
The *Daily Telegraph* 1990.
The *Falkirk Herald* 1939-1945.
The *Stirling Observer* 1939-1945.
The *Haddingtonshire Courier* 1940-1941.
The *Perthshire Advertiser* 1938.
The *Glasgow Herald* 1938-1941.
Anglo-German Review 1938-1940.
Vanguard 1943-1944.

Acknowledgments

This book could not have been written without the help of many organisations and individuals. Edinburgh District Council Archives gave me access to files, most of which had lain unseen for 50 years or more. Huntly House Museum and the Scottish United Services Museum provided invaluable material and photographs. Also in Edinburgh, resources provided by both the Central Library and the National Library of Scotland place me in their debt. I am also grateful to Scotsman Publications Ltd and George Outram & Co. Ltd (publishers of the *Herald* and *Evening Times* in Glasgow) for permission to use their photographs, Central Regional Council Archives Department, Falkirk and Paisley Museums, the Mitchell Library in Glasgow and the Scottish Record Office.

In London, the British Newspaper Library at Colindale and the Departments of Photographs and Printed Books at the Imperial War Museum were, as ever, courteous and helpful.

The largest single source of research material on the Second World War is the Public Record Office at Kew. For this book I have examined Home Office and Cabinet papers on the Ramsay affair; Air Ministry, War Office and Admiralty papers on the military war; Ministry of Information and Ministry of Home Security papers on the Home Front. My thanks go not only to the staff of the PRO but also to those unsung military personnel and civil servants who laboured long to keep their war diaries up to date, often in trying circumstances.

I have been singularly fortunate in being able to call on the memories of so many of those who took part in the incidents described. Others were kind enough to give me access to research material laboriously collected over many years. It is unfortunate that, in thanking them all, I can only make particular mention of a few.

I am grateful to His Grace the Earl of Elgin, Air Vice-Marshal Sandy Johnstone, Group Captain George Denholm, Group Captain George Pinkerton, Wing-Commander Hector MacLean, Squadron-Leader Bruce Blanche, for access to his extensive archive of 603 Squadron material, Pilot Officer Glen Niven, Ralph Burnett, Dugald Cameron and Alastair Carswell of Squadron Prints, Herr Helmut Pohle, John Dickson, Ian McGarrity, Jack Smith, Mrs Margaret Sands, Bill Harkness, John Guy of the Fortress Study Group, Bob Baird, Adam McNaughtan, George Jackson and many others whose contributions, great or small, went towards this book. I am greatly in their debt.